Abstracts
and the
Writing of Abstracts

JOHN M. SWALES
CHRISTINE B. FEAK

VOLUME 1 OF THE REVISED AND EXPANDED EDITION OF
English in Today's Research World

 The Michigan Series in English for
Academic & Professional Purposes

ISBN-13: 978-0-472-03335-5

2020   2019   2018   2017   6   5   4   3

Acknowledgments

We have been helped in the devising of this first small volume in the new series by a considerable number of people. First, we would like to thank all the participants in our advanced writing classes, workshops, and seminars who have provided us in recent years with evaluations and suggestions for improving our materials. In addition to those at the University of Michigan, these include staff and students at the School of Economics and Political Science at Waseda University in Tokyo, post-doctoral fellows at the Perinatology Research Branch at Wayne State University in Detroit, the staff and students at the Federal University in Santa Maria (Brazil), and the English faculty at Madrid Polytechnic University.

We are also very grateful to those who have been willing to allow their own texts to be used as illustrative materials, whether under their own names or anonymously. We are much indebted to Nicole Robidoux of the library of the English Language Institute at the University of Michigan for her excellent and efficient work in obtaining permissions to use published abstracts. This volume wouldn't have been completed in such a timely manner and with so few glitches without the help of our two research assistants. First, our thanks go to Rebecca Maybaum for cataloging mounds of disorganized teaching materials and for using her corpus linguistics skills to check and modify many of our statements about research English. Second, we owe even more to Vera Irwin, for her care and attention to the evolving manuscript, for her critical insights, and for her contributions to the main volume and to the accompanying Commentary. Rebecca has now gone off to graduate school in the U.K., but we hope Vera will continue to assist us in the volumes to come.

We are highly appreciative of the comments and observations made by the two anonymous reviewers; indeed, we have adopted nearly all of their suggestions. We have also received much interesting data and many good ideas from Dr. An Cheng of Oklahoma State University, and we owe the "checklist" concept to Dr. Jane Freeman of Toronto University. Our EAP colleagues at the English Language Institute have continued to be as supportive as ever. We also owe a great deal to Kelly Sippell of the University of

Michigan Press, who, over the years, has not only become a good friend but also a great editor in the fields of ESL and Applied Linguistics. Her continuing support for us both as authors and as editors of the EAPP series has been invaluable.

Finally, on a more personal level, John would like to express his deep appreciation to Vi Benner, who quickly came to realize that for John retirement "would just be a name," and that any hopes for improvements around the house would have to wait. (Alas, the bathroom still badly needs painting.) Chris would like to express her appreciation to Glen for his support of her seemingly endless list of projects.

JMS & CBF

Ann Arbor

January 2009

Grateful acknowledgment is made to the following authors, publishers, and journals for permission to reprint previously published materials.

Alberta Journal of Educational Research for abstract that appeared with "Antiracist/Multicultural Teacher Education: A Focus on Student Teachers. Research Notes" by Jon Young and Nancy Buchanan, Vol. 42, No. 1 (1996): 60–64.

American Journal of Perinatology for abstract that appeared with "Psychiatric Symptoms among Postpartum Women in an Urban Hospital Setting" by Ivan L. Hand, Vol. 23, No. 6 (Aug. 14, 2006): 329–34.

Blackwell Publishing for abstract that appeared in *American Journal of Political Science,* "Is Democracy Good for the Poor?" by Michael Ross, Vol. 50, No. 1 (2006): 860–74.

Elsevier Ltd. for abstract that appeared in *Human Resource Management Review,* "Taxonomic Model of Withdrawal Behaviors: The Adaptive Response Model" by Rodger W. Griffeth, Stephan Gaertner, and Jeffrey K. Sager, Vol. 9, No. 4 (1999): 577–90. Reprinted with permission.

Emerald Group Publishing Limited for abstract that appeared in *Accounting, Auditing & Accountability Journal,* "Household Accounting in Australia: Prescription and Practice from the 1820s to the 1960s" by Garry D. Carnegie and Stephen P. Walker, Vol. 20, No. 1 (2007): 41–73; www.emerald insight.com/Insight/ViewContentServlet?Filename=Published/ EmeraldFullTextArticle/Articles/0590200102.html.

IOP Publishing Limited for abstract that appeared in *Measurement Science and Technology,* "A Novel Application of Speckle Interferometry for the Measurement of Strain Distributions in Semi-Sweet Biscuits" by Q. Saleem et al., Vol. 14 (2003).

Journal of the Medical Library Association for abstract that appeared with "Current Findings from Research on Structured Abstracts" by James Hartley, Vol. 92, No. 3 (2004): 368–71.

Journal of Navigation for abstract that appeared with "Collision Rules for High-Speed Craft" by Dag Pike, Vol. 58, No. 1 (2005): 159–63.

Latin American Journal of Nursing for abstract that appeared with "The Importance of Bucal Health for Adolescents of Different Social Strata of Ribeirao Preto" by Marina Sa Elias, Maria Aparecida Tedeschi Cano, Wilson Mestriner Junior et al., Vol. 9, No. 1 (2001): 88–95.

The Ornithological Society of New Zealand, Inc., for abstract that appeared in *Notornis,* "The Occurrence of Owls in the Marshall Islands" by Dirk H.R. Spennemann, Vol. 51 (2004): 147–51.

Every effort has been made to contact the copyright holders for permissions to reprint borrowed material. We regret any oversights that may have occurred and will rectify them in future printings of this book.

Contents

General Introduction to the Volumes   ix
Introduction to the Abstracts Volume   xiii
    A Crucial First Step   xiv

Research Article (RA) Abstracts   1
    General Analysis of RA Abstracts   3
    Specific Analyses   9
       Getting Started (Moves 1 and 2)   9
       Language Focus: Links between S1 and S2   11
       Compressing Methods Descriptions (Move 3)   14
       Moving On: Results (Move 4)   16
       Language Focus: Main Results and *That* Clauses in
          Traditional Abstracts   18
       Concluding a Traditional Abstract (Move 5)   21
       A Final Issue: A Need to Problematize in the Abstract?   23
    Structured Research Article Abstracts   26
       Statements of Objective   28
       Language Focus: Opening the Conclusion Section   32

Abstracts for Short Communications   35

Conference Abstracts   43
    A Closer Look at the Organization of Conference Abstracts   45
    The Rating of Conference Abstracts   51
    The Role of a Senior Author: An Example   52
    The Problem of Promissory Abstracts   55
    Conference Abstract Titles   57
    Structured Conference Abstracts   60
    Conference Program Abstracts or Summaries   63

PhD Dissertation Abstracts   67

Choosing Keywords   79

Appendix: Notes on Cross-Linguistic Issues   81
Sources   85
References   87

General Introduction to the Volumes

John and Chris first started putting together the book that became *English in Today's Research World: A Writing Guide* (henceforth *ETRW*)in early 1998. The book was largely based on teaching materials we had been developing through the 1990s for our advanced courses in dissertation writing and writing for publication at the University of Michigan. Ten years later, that "research world" and our understanding of its texts and discourses have both changed considerably. This revised and expanded series of volumes is an attempt to respond to those changes. It also attempts to respond to reactions to *ETRW* that have come from instructors and users and that have reached us directly, or through Kelly Sippell, ESL Editor at the University of Michigan Press. One consistent feature of these comments has been that *ETRW* is somewhat unwieldy because it contains too many disparate topics. In thinking about a second edition, therefore, we have made the radical decision to break the original book into several small volumes; in addition, we offer a volume principally designed for instructors and tutors of research English and for those who wish to enter this growing field of specialization. We hope in this way that instructors or independent researcher-users can choose those volumes that are most directly relevant to their own situations at any particular time.

However, we do need to stress that many of the genres we separately deal with are inter-connected. Abstracts are always abstracts of some larger text. A conference talk may be based on a dissertation chapter and may end up as an article. Grant proposals lead to technical reports, to dissertations, and to further grant proposals. To indicate these inter-connected networks, the genre network diagram (see Figure 1) we used in *ETRW* is even more appropriate and relevant to this multi-volume series.

One continuing development in the research world has been the increasing predominance of English as the vehicle for communicating research findings. Of late, this trend has been reinforced by policy decisions made by ministries of higher education, universities, and research centers that researchers and scholars will primarily receive credit for publications appearing in English-medium international journals, especially those that are

Figure 1. Academic Genre Network

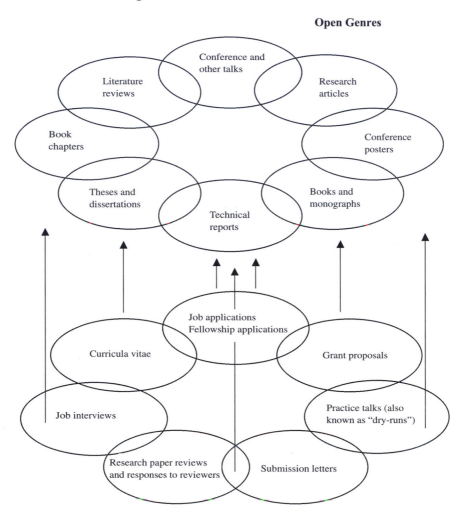

included in the Institute for Scientific Information (ISI) database. Indeed, in recent years, the range of "acceptable" outlets has often further narrowed to those ISI journals that have a high impact factor (in other words, those with numerous citations to articles published over the previous three years). Selected countries around the world that have apparently adopted this kind of policy include Spain, the United Kingdom, China, Brazil, Malaysia, Chile, and Sri Lanka. Competition to publish in these high-status restricted outlets is obviously increasingly tough, and the pressures on academics to publish therein are often unreasonable. A further complicating development has been the rise and spread of the so-called "article-compilation" PhD thesis or dissertation in which the candidate is expected to have an article or two published in international journals *before* graduation.

The increasing number of people in today's Anglophone research world who do not have English as their first language has meant that the traditional distinction between native speakers and non-native speakers (NNS) of English is collapsing. A number of scholars have rightly argued that we need to get rid of this discriminatory division and replace NNS with speakers of English as a lingua franca (ELF) or speakers of English as an additional language (EAL). Today, the more valid and valuable distinctions are between senior researchers and junior researchers, on the one hand, and between those who have a broad proficiency in research English across the four skills of reading, writing, listening, and speaking and those with a narrow proficiency largely restricted to the written mode, on the other.

There have also been important developments in English for Academic Purposes (EAP) and allied fields. The relevant journals have been full of articles analyzing research English, often discussing as well the pedagogical consequences of such studies. This has been particularly true of studies emanating from Spain. Indeed, the first international conference on "Publishing and presenting research internationally" was held in January 2007 at La Laguna University in the Canary Islands. The use of corpus linguistic techniques applied to specialized electronic databases or corpora has been on the rise. The number of specialized courses and workshops has greatly expanded, partly as a way of utilizing this new knowledge but more significantly as a response to the increasing demand. Finally, information is much more widely available on the Internet about academic and research English, particularly via search engines such as Google Scholar. As is our custom, we have made much use of relevant research findings in these volumes, and we—and our occasional research assistants—have undertaken discoursal studies when we found gaps in the research literature. In this process, we have also made use of a number of specialized corpora, including Ken Hyland's corpus of 240 research articles spread across eight disciplines and two others we have constructed at Michigan (one of Dental research articles and the other of research articles from Perinatology and ultrasound research).

In this new venture, we have revised—often extensively—material from the original textbook, deleting texts and activities that we feel do not work so well and adding new material, at least partly in response to the developments mentioned earlier in this introduction. One concept, however, that we have retained from our previous textbooks is in-depth examinations of specific language options at what seem particularly appropriate points.

As this and other volumes begin to appear, we are always interested in user response, and so we welcome comments at either or both cfeak@umich.edu or jmswales@umich.edu.

Introduction to the Abstracts Volume

"I would have written a shorter letter, but I did not have the time."

—Blaise Pascal, French philosopher, 1657

A variety of abstracts and summaries are widely used in the research world. In this small volume, we aim to offer help with the composing of most of them. Abstracts typically have restrictions with regard to the number of words, and these limits make the already difficult task of constructing abstracts even harder. Even experienced and widely published authors usually have to produce several versions before they are satisfied that they have summarized their longer texts with maximum efficiency, clarity, and economy.

This book therefore is designed to help graduate students and junior researchers with their abstracts. In addition, some tasks in this volume have been designed with the needs of those whose mother tongue is not English in mind. The book, or relevant parts of it, can be used in advanced writing classes, in workshops, or in seminars, or it can be used by individuals working on their own. With the last group particularly in mind, the *Commentary* offers possible answers to the less open tasks and some further notes on relevant points (see www.press.umich.edu/esl/compsite/ETRW/.)

The approach we have adopted in this new series is broadly the same as that used in our earlier textbooks: *Academic Writing for Graduate Students* (2d ed., 2004) and *English in Today's Research World: A Writing Guide* (1998). This can be summarized by this simple wheel diagram:

Figure 2. The Four-A Wheel

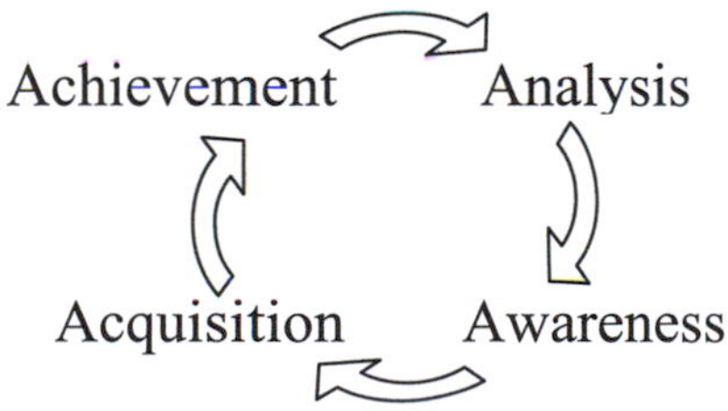

Achievement   Analysis

Acquisition   Awareness

We know that users of this volume will be highly educated and will have developed high levels of analytic skills in their own disciplinary fields. We make use of these skills by asking you to undertake various kinds of linguistic and rhetorical analysis, often by comparing some features of a text from a different field with what you know or can discover about texts in your own area. We believe that these comparisons lead to a greater awareness and understanding of how research English is constructed, which then provide a platform for further acquisition of specific writing skills. These in turn lead to your texts becoming more easily acceptable to members of your target disciplinary community or communities.

A Crucial First Step

Okay, you have to write an abstract. You perhaps need to do this to accompany a journal article, or to submit an abstract for an upcoming conference, or you have nearly finished your thesis or dissertation. Alternatively, you have been accepted for a conference (congratulations!), and you now have to come up with a short version to be published in the program.

Naturally, the first step is to find out how many words (or sometimes characters) you have to work with. Here are some general guidelines for four different types of abstract:

- Most journals seem to ask for between 150 and 200 words for traditional abstracts (i.e., for those without subheadings). Structured abstracts—those divided into a number of named sections—can be longer. For example, the publishers of *Emerald Journals*, which require structured abstracts for all the articles they publish—have a maximum limit of 250 words.[1]
- Abstracts for U.S. PhD dissertations should not exceed 350 words.
- Conference submission abstracts in some fields may be longer, 500 words or more.

---

[1] Traditional and structured abstracts are just the names for two abstract formats. We, of course, do not wish to imply that traditional abstracts are somehow "unstructured." Emerald celebrated its 40th anniversary in 2007 and publishes more than 180 journals, mostly in management fields.

- The IEEE (Institute of Electrical and Electronics Engineers) asks for 50-word abstracts for "short communications" published in its many journals. Published conference program abstracts can also be as short as this.

This list of guidelines, of course, offers only generalizations. In any particular case, you need to check the word—or character—limits. These days, the simplest way to do this is to go to the appropriate website. If you might be submitting a manuscript to a journal, don't forget to check whether a structured abstract is required.

In this volume, we will deal with traditional research article (RA) abstracts first, followed by a shorter section on structured abstracts. Then we will move on to conference abstracts and short program summaries. These in turn are followed by a quick look at dissertation abstracts. Toward the end we deal with titles, the ordering of author names, and keywords. We will not be dealing with abstracts found in abstracting journals or databases such as MEDLINE in the medical field or LLBA in our own field of language studies. Many of these use special conventions and are typically prepared by professional abstract writers. Therefore, they are beyond the scope of this volume. We also do not deal in this volume with abstracts or summaries accompanying research grant proposals.

Research Article (RA) Abstracts

The research world is facing "an information explosion" with several million research papers being published each year. There are also continual announcements of new journals being launched, either online or in hard copy or both. Many researchers, therefore, have to be highly selective in their reading, often focusing on skimming abstracts and key words. Research article (RA) abstracts have thus become an increasingly important part-genre.[1] In the "old days," most papers did not have abstracts; surprisingly perhaps, abstracts were only introduced into medical research articles during the 1960s. And the now-fashionable so-called "structured" abstract (i.e., with named subsections) did not appear until about 1987.

---

[1] *Genre* is a name for a type of text or discourse designed to achieve a set of communicative purposes. Following this terminology, the research article is a genre, and various parts of it, such as the Abstract and Discussion, are part-genres.

For some top journals such as the *British Medical Journal (BMJ)* and the *Journal of the American Medical Association (JAMA)*, the acceptance rate for RA manuscripts is typically about 5 percent. Among journals such as these, manuscripts may be rejected after a reading of the abstract alone (Langdon-Neuner, 2008). While we need to stress that such rejections will be largely based on the perceived scientific merit of the paper (or lack thereof), it remains the case that a careful and coherent abstract can only help a manuscript reach the next step of external review.

According to Huckin (2001), RA abstracts have at least four distinguishable functions:

1. They function as stand-alone *mini-texts,* giving readers a short summary of a study's topic, methodology, and main findings

2. They function as *screening devices,* helping readers decide whether they wish to read the whole article or not

3. They function as *previews* for readers intending to read the whole article, giving them a road-map for their reading

4. They provide *indexing help* for professional abstract writers and editors

In addition, there are suggestions, at least in the medical literature (e.g., Bordage & McGaghie, 2001), that:

5. They provide *reviewers with an immediate oversight* of the paper they have been asked to review

Task One

Rank these five functions in terms of their importance to you and your field. Are there any that you think are irrelevant? Are there any other functions that you can think of? Does this task change your own approach to constructing abstracts in any way? (Sample answers for the tasks in the RA section can be found in the *Commentary* at www.press.umich.edu/esl/compsite/ETRW/.)

General Analysis of RA Abstracts

For this part of the book, you will need to put together a small reference collection (10–15 examples) of abstracts from a suitable journal or journals in your own field. We suggest that you take recent issues, and perhaps those in electronic format so that the texts can be copied and pasted for analysis. This collection of part-genres will be your reference corpus, a corpus being an accumulation of texts used for study and analysis.

We suggest that you do this mainly because a number of the following activities ask you to compare data or texts we present with those that are most relevant to you. For example, there are several questions of this type in the next task. So you need to put your reference collection together before you attempt Task Two.

Task Two

Read this traditional (unstructured) abstract from political science, and answer the questions that follow. Sentence numbers have been added for your convenience.

Abstract

① Many scholars claim that democracy improves the welfare of the poor. ② This article uses data on infant and child mortality[a] to challenge this claim. ③ Cross-national studies tend to exclude from their samples non-democratic states that have performed well; this leads to the mistaken inference that non-democracies have worse records than democracies. ④ Once these and other flaws[b] are corrected, democracy has little or no effect on infant and child mortality rates. ⑤ Democracies spend more money on education and health than non-democracies, but these benefits seem to accrue to middle- and upper-income groups.

Notes
[a] the percentage death rate
[b] errors

1. Underline what you consider to be the key clause (or part-sentence) in the abstract.

2. This opening abstract has five sentences and contains only 91 words. Thus, it is (deliberately) shorter than average.

Now consider this data:

Table 1: RA Abstracts from Various Fields, adapted from Orasan (2001)

Field	# of Sentences	Average # of Words
Computer Science	9.6	232
Chemistry	8.6	215
Artificial Intelligence	8.2	166
Biology	7.9	196
Anthropology	6.2	158
Linguistics	5.8	150
Overall Averages	**7.4**	**175**

Here are two questions based on Table 1:

a. What patterns do you notice in this table?

b. Where would you guess your field might fit in the table? (If it is not one of these.)

3. What is the main tense used in this abstract? Why is this tense used? What is typical in your field? Check your reference collection.

4. This abstract uses no citations or references to previous research. Is this typical in your experience?

5. Does the abstract author use *I* or *we?* What is your experience here? Refer to your reference collection. Does your field commonly use expressions like *the present authors?*

6. In the abstract, there is a single "self-referring" or "metadiscoursal" expression.[2] In this case it is *this article* in Sentence 2. Are metadiscoursal expressions used in abstracts in your field? If so, what are the common nouns?

7. Are acronyms/abbreviations used in the example abstract? In your field, do they occur? And if so, of what kind?

---

[2] *Metadiscourse* is a common concept in studies of academic texts. It has various definitions. In this series, we use a narrow definition of "text about your text," as in ***In the following section,*** *we offer a computer simulation.*

8. Much recent work in discourse analysis has investigated the number of "rhetorical moves"[3] (or communicative stages) in abstracts in various fields—and in various languages. Most researchers identify a *potential* total of five moves. Terminology varies somewhat, but these are in their typical order as follows:

Move #	Typical Labels	Implied questions
Move 1	Background/introduction/ situation	What do we know about the topic? Why is the topic important?
Move 2	Present research/purpose	What is this study about?
Move 3	Methods/materials/ subjects/procedures	How was it done?
Move 4	Results/findings	What was discovered?
Move 5	Discussion/conclusion/ implications/ recommendations	What do the findings mean?

In the abstract on page 3, how many of these five moves can you find? And what are they?

Earlier we said that abstracts have a potential maximum of these five moves. As we will see later, Moves 4 and 2 are most common, and Move 5 is the least common.

[3] A *move* is a stretch of text that does a particular job. It is a functional, not a grammatical term. A move can vary in length from a phrase to a paragraph.

Task Three

Here are four more RA abstracts. Choose the one closest to your own area, and analyze it in terms of the eight questions from Task Two. We repeat these for you in summary form here.

1. Key clause?

2. In terms of Table 1, is your chosen abstract of expected length or not?

3. Most common verb tense?

4. Any citations?

5. Any first-person pronouns?

6. Any metadiscourse?

7. Any acronyms and abbreviations?

8. Move structure? (If you are unsure about this, look at the blocked text on page 9.)

1. *Psychology*

① This article presents and develops a theoretical model (The Adaptive Response Model; ARM) that proposes how employees adapt to the organization following changes in organizational policies that are perceived as dissatisfying. ② The ARM combines several streams of theoretical and empirical research in IO-Psychology. ③ It suggests that different type of employees (i.e., institutionalized stars, citizens, lone wolves, and apathetics) resort to different behaviors to adjust to dissatisfying events. ④ Institutionalized stars tend to exercise voice, lone wolves tend to exit, citizens tend to accept, and apathetics tend to resort to alternative forms of withdrawal (e.g., lateness, absenteeism, and theft). ⑤ Implications for the management of each employee type as well as suggestions for future research are discussed.[4]

---

[4] For more explanation of terminology used in this abstract, see the Commentary on Task Three.

2. *Education*

①Prekindergarten programs are expanding rapidly but evidence on their effects is limited. ② Using rich data from Early Childhood Longitudinal Study, we estimate the effects of prekindergarten on children's school readiness. ③ We find that prekindergarten is associated with higher reading and mathematics skills at school entry, but also higher levels of behavior problems. ④ By the spring of first grade, estimated effects on academic skills have largely dissipated, but the behavioral effects persist. ⑤ Larger and longer lasting associations with academic gains are found for disadvantaged children. ⑥ Finally, we find some evidence that prekindergartens located in public schools do not have adverse effects on behavior problems.

3. *Mechanical Engineering and Food Service*

① The spontaneous formation of cracks in biscuits following baking, also known as checking, is an issue that manufacturers would like to be able to predict and avoid. ② Unfortunately the mechanisms driving this phenomenon are not well understood. ③ Speckle interferometry was used to study moisture-induced in-plane strain development in biscuits. ④ This sensitive and non-contacting technique for measuring surface displacements has two major advantages over more commonly used methods; firstly, strains can be detected at a far higher sensitivity (down to 2×10^{-6}) than previously accessible and secondly the method is a whole-field technique, enabling observation of the development of strain distributions during moisture migration. ⑤ For biscuits exposed to step changes in humidity, initial strain rates of up to 10^{-5}min^{-1} were measured, which decreased as the moisture content approached equilibrium, leading to an accumulated strain of $\sim 10^{-2}$ after 48 h. ⑥ Under these conditions, a homogeneous, uniform strain distribution was observed. ⑦ The data were used to calculate the hygroscopic expansion coefficient, which was linearly related to moisture content and provides the necessary constitutive link between strain and biscuit moisture content needed to model biscuit checking.

4. *Art History*

① By way of a case study devoted to Jean-Jacques Hauer (1751–1829), one of the minor figures making their Salon[a] debut in the French Revolution, this essay explores the relations between art and historical events in times of radical transformation. ② A citizen-artist serving with the National Guard, the painter was a humble practitioner enjoying his greatest success at the height of collective militancy known as the *sans-culotte*[b] movement. ③ The French Revolution allowed Hauer to go public, and most of his œuvre is closely tied to its tangled politics. ④ Representations from the death of Marat to the plight of the royal family are examined in the context of shifting discourses, sectionary politics and civic commitment.

Notes
[a] the annual art exhibition in Paris
[b] without the knee-length trousers worn by men from the upper classes (i.e., popular republican movement of the poorer classes)

Look over a subset of abstracts in your corpus, and answer the eight questions for your own field of study.

Now that we have obtained a general sense of the shape of abstracts, we can turn to how specific moves are realized in each move.

Specific Analyses

Getting Started (Moves 1 and 2)

We will explore this issue by taking the case of RA abstracts in one of the medical fields. The field we have chosen is Perinatology. Perinatology, also known as Maternal-Fetal medicine, deals with high-risk pregnancies and has a number of research journals. Some of these require structured abstracts, and some continue to use traditional ones. As a preview, here is a typical traditional abstract from this field. We have blocked it into moves for you. *Postpartum* means "after having given birth."

Abstract

① The object of this study was to evaluate postpartum women for psychiatric symptomatology including cognitive disturbances, anxiety, depression, and anger to better meet their needs for support and involve them in the care of their infants. **Move 2**

② We interviewed 52 postpartum mothers at the Bronx Lebanon Hospital Center within 5 days of delivery and determined the presence of psychiatric symptoms using the 29-item Psychiatric Symptom Index. **Move 3**

③ Despite the fact that adult mothers were happier when they were pregnant (71.4% versus 29.4%; $p = 0.010$) and less likely to be worried about their baby's health (25.7% versus 52.9%; $p = 0.003$), adult mothers demonstrated higher depressive symptomatology ($p = 0.009$), higher amounts of anger ($p = 0.004$), and greater overall psychiatric symptomatology ($p = 0.005$) than adolescent mothers. ④ Mothers whose infants were in the neonatal intensive care unit did not report significantly higher psychiatric symptomatology than mothers whose infants were healthy. **Move 4**

⑤ Physicians need to be aware of the high levels of depression and anger present among postpartum women so appropriate support can be given. **Move 5**

1. In the Results move (Move 4), the significant findings in Sentence 3 are given before those that are not significant in Sentence 4.

2. The question of tense in purpose/objective/object statements in abstracts and introductions often arises. A general rule is that if a **genre-name** is used (e.g., the purpose of this *paper/article* . . .) the present tense is chosen, but if a noun is used that describes **the type of investigation** *(The purpose of this experiment / survey / analysis)*, the past tense is preferred. With the rather vague term *study*—a very common choice in some fields—it would seem that the past tense is generally preferred, especially in the life and health sciences, but even there some exceptions can be found.

3. Note that in this and other medical fields, Move 5 quite often takes the form of a recommendation.

After this analysis of a single abstract, we now need to have a broader look at how abstracts get started.

Our research suggests that there are four basic types of opening sentences. We illustrate these with simple examples from economics.

Type A: Starting with a Real-World Phenomenon or with Standard Practice

Corporate taxation rates vary around the world.

Economists have long been interested in the relationship between corporate taxation and corporate strategy.

Type B: Starting with Purpose or Objective

The aim of this study is to examine the effects of the recent change in corporate taxation.

Type C: Starting with Present Researcher Action

We analyze corporate taxation returns before and after the introduction of the new tax rules.

Type D: Starting with a Problem or an Uncertainty

The relationship between corporate taxation and corporate strategy remain unclear.

Task Four

1. Make up from your own area of research another example opening sentence for each of the four opening types.

2. Now look at the opening sentences in your own reference corpus of abstracts. How many fall in each type? Do you need any new types? Is there a type you did not find? Be prepared to comment on your findings.

(Of the first 20 abstracts in our Perinatology corpus, ten opened with Type A, eight with Type B, two with Type C, and none with Type D. This distribution did not surprise us.)

Language Focus: Links between Sentence 1 and Sentence 2

We have already suggested that the moves tend to follow a set sequence. For example, *purpose/objective* openings in perinatology are typically followed by sentences describing *researcher action*. So far, so good. However, we can also examine the relationship between the opening sentences in another way. We can see how the second sentence is grammatically linked—or not linked—to the first.

Research suggests that there are basically three options:

1. keep roughly the same subject *(continuing subject)*
2. put the information from the second half of the first sentence in the subject position at the beginning of the second *(capturing subject)*
3. use a new previously unmentioned topic as subject *(new subject)*

To see how this works out, let us reconsider the eight instances of *purpose* openings we found in Perinatology:

1. Continuing Subject

1. *The purpose of this study* was to analyze the influence of . . . on mortality . . .
2. *This* was a multicenter, prospective, observational study.

We can see here that the authors have in Sentence 2 commented further on the methodological nature of their study, using *this* as the subject. Two of the eight examples used this way of connecting the two sentences.

2. Capturing Subject

1. The purpose of this study was to identify risk factors and to characterize *infants with respiratory distress syndrome (RDS)*.

2. *A total of 67 newborns with RDS*, born at gestational age (GA) > 35 weeks, were studied.

In this case, the authors have picked up the information toward the end of Sentence 1—typically new information—and repackaged it at the onset of Sentence 2. We have called this a *capturing* grammatical subject. Four of the eight examples used this type of link.

3. New Subject

1. The objective of this study was to define the variables associated with vaginal birth after cesarean section (VBAC) and to . . .

2. *We* searched our computerized database for parturients with a history of VBAC. . . .

In this case, the *we* subject introduced a new grammatical entity into the text. There were two of these.

In general, new sentence subjects (i.e., "jumping" subjects) are in fact quite common in abstracts for a number of reasons:

- Abstracts have strict word limits.
- Abstracts are highly compressed texts.
- Authors expect readers to have considerable relevant content knowledge.
- Experienced readers' expectations of how abstracts will develop are well established.

Additionally, we note that the increasing use of structured abstracts (see the next section) may increase this "jumping" effect.

Task Five

Here we provide three abstract opening sentences, each from a different field. In each case, the opening sentence is followed by three alternative second sentences.

1. Identify whether these second sentences are *continuing*, *capturing*, or *new*.

2. Be prepared to explain which second sentence you prefer and perhaps why.

Engineering

1. The objective of this paper is to examine the flapping characteristics of insect wings.
   a) This objective was realized through the use of two high-speed video cameras.
   b) These characteristics were studied through the use of two high-speed video cameras.
   c) For this purpose, we utilized two high-speed video cameras.

Higher Education

2. As yet, little is known about the information-seeking characteristics of today's undergraduate students.
   a) The current study thus sought to gain an understanding of student information-seeking habits and preferences.
   b) Identification of such characteristics would have several beneficial effects such as more efficient assignment design.
   c) This lack of knowledge is impeding optimal delivery of library services.

Sociology

3. A general international observation is that adolescents from disadvantaged families are more likely to leave school at or before 16.
   a) In this paper, we extend this literature by using a new dataset from New Zealand.
   b) Such observations have, however, been largely derived from research conducted in the northern hemisphere.
   c) Early school-leaving decisions typically have adverse consequences for lifetime income.

Compressing Methods Descriptions (Move 3)

After all this work on openings (Move 1 and 2), it is time to consider methods (Move 3).

Move 3 can include information about data, participants, length of study, location, etc., as well as some indication of the methods used themselves. In other words, a lot of information needs to be packed into a small space.

Unless the contribution made by the paper lies principally in the methodology, method descriptions in RA abstracts may have to be squeezed to make room for more information in other moves. Also, in general, methods moves are more likely to use past tense and the passive.

Now consider the following situation.

A research group has written this opening to a draft RA abstract. The group is reporting on a relatively large-scale study in the field of business communications.

Abstract

① Increasing globalization is thought to be impacting business communications around the world (e.g., Connor, 2004). ② To assess possible impacts in one developing country, we examine contemporary written business communications in Turkey.

So far, so good. Now for Move 3 (Method, etc.). So far the group has reduced the data/methods write-up in the draft article to the following summary:

③ The primary data used consist of approximately 300 memoranda (internal correspondence) and 150 fax messages (external correspondence) associated with four different Turkish companies selected to represent a range of sectors, sizes and management styles. ④ Analysis of the primary data was supported by interviews with executives from these four companies. (50 words)

"Still too long," they conclude, because the allowed maximum for their entire abstract is only 100 words. So each of the three members attempts a further reduction.

Task Six

Which of the three alternatives do you prefer, and why? Work in pairs if possible. Can you come up with an even better fourth version (of no more than 25 words)?

Sunil's version

③ The primary data consist of internal and external correspondence (faxes) from four very different Turkish companies. ④ Secondary data comes from interviews with selected executives. (24 words)

Didar's version

③ The main data consists of 300 memoranda and 150 faxes associated with four Turkish companies representing a range of different types of enterprise. (22 words)

Cengiz's version

③ Internal memoranda and external faxes were collected from four Turkish companies of varying sizes. ④ This primary data was supported by secondary interviews. (22 words)

Task Seven

The advisor has told this doctoral student in workplace ergonomics that her draft RA abstract is unbalanced because too much space is given to methods. Reduce the draft to no more than 30 words. The opening of the abstract had stressed the need for further research into health consequences of poorly designed computer workstations.

② In a 14-week experiment, a total of 78 workers were asked to test keyboarding in alternating positions (between sitting and standing). ③ There were two types of modified workstation (ALT1 and ALT2) in contrast to the sit-only position of their original workstations. ④ ALT1 allowed keying in both sitting and standing positions, while ALT2 allowed only a standing position. (59 words)

Moving On: Results (Move 4)

Before we explore this key move in some detail, we might here ask the question "When is the best time to write the abstract of an RA?" One obvious answer would be once the first draft of the article is completed, but there is another possibility. Consider this study:

Arthur H. Compton won the Nobel Prize for physics in 1927. In 1923, he published a famous paper providing the first empirical verification of quantum theory. His discovery has since been known as the Compton Effect. Charles Bazerman (1988) made a detailed study of Compton's manuscripts and notes and found that Compton apparently wrote the abstract about two-thirds of the way through the manuscript. Bazerman writes, "he felt he needed to write the abstract before completing the article, in order to articulate his sense of the whole and to keep the later parts logically and structurally consistent" (1988: 221). You might like to consider Compton's strategy.

Now let us turn our attention to the results. Two questions may arise when we think about how to present the results of a study to the abstract reader:

1. How do you organize your findings? Do you first talk about results in general? Do you then provide specific information about your findings?

2. For quantitative studies, do you precise numbers and percentages in your abstract or is it better to provide an approximation of your results?

To answer these questions, we looked at 20 abstracts from four disciplines: Education, Economics, Dentistry, and Microbiology.

As for Question 1 (and as expected), across disciplines, a general tendency was to present the general results first, followed by the specifics, such as in:

Economics

Firstly, the EPI of Korea is more affected by other countries than those of the USA and Japan. Specifically, Korean economic growth and the balance of payments are largely affected by Japan.

Microbiology

The data confirmed the results of sensory evaluations and showed the ability of wild lactobacilli to generate key volatile compounds. Particularly, three wild lactobacilli strains. . . .

(And note the common use of adverbs such as *particularly* and *specifically* to indicate the transition from general to specific.)

In two of the twenty cases, however, the discussion of the specific results in the abstract was *followed* by a short result summary, pointing out a general trend or summarizing author's observations, such as:

Education

There are three major findings. First, . . . Second, . . . Third, . . . In sum, high quality teacher-child relationships fostered children's achievement.

Dentistry

[Specific results are first, then . . .] The combined results for all treatment steps showed a significant difference between the methods for the CIE L* values.[a]

Note

[a] Commission International de l'Eclairage (or International Commission on Illumination) lightness values, which range from 0 (black) to 100 (white)

(Note the use of *in sum;* other ways of indicating generality are *in general, overall, more generally.*)

As for the second question, the abstracts for all the quantitative studies analyzed provided exact numbers and exact statistical data on the findings. Abstract authors presumably did this in order to stress the precision of their work. As the saying goes, perhaps "numbers speak louder than words"?

Language Focus: Main Results and
That Clauses in Traditional Abstracts

Hyland and Tse (2005) examined 240 abstracts spread across six fields covering a wide spectrum of disciplines. They found that, on average, *that* clauses occurred 1.2 times per abstract. This finding is not, in itself, significant. What is significant, however, is that as many as 88 percent of the 272 clauses found were used to describe the article authors' *own findings* as part of Move 4.

In effect, the abstract writers were using these *that* clauses to give the major details of their own results while prefacing them with an evaluative main clause. And here there was a strong tendency to use an inanimate subject *(The results . . . The findings of this study)* rather than a human subject *(We . . . I)*.[5] Here are two examples:

- *This research shows that* junior scholars often need help with their abstracts.
- *The results offer clear evidence that* global warming is a reality.

The use of such sentences operates to highlight the key findings of the study, while allowing authors, with their choice of reporting verb, to indicate the strength of claim from strong (e.g., *prove*) to weak (e.g., *suggest*).

---

[5] In Hyland and Tse's data, the computer science abstracts constituted an exception to this generalization, where personal pronoun subjects were common. Hyland & Tse's six fields did not include one from the medical or dental fields; Chris's own research suggests that these *that* statements are not so common in these areas.

Task Eight

Convert five of these noun phrases into appropriate *that* clauses. Some of the later ones are not so easy to convert! Here is an example:

The results offer clear evidence of the reality of global warming.

The results offer clear evidence that global warming is a reality.

1. Results confirm the influence of year of study and academic discipline on student information choices.

2. The evidence shows a primary association between the word *elderly* and discourses of care and disability.

3. The analysis indicates the dependence of the peak pressure of shock waves on the deformation speed of the overlays.

4. The findings generally support the idea of a profitable introduction of structured abstracts into research journals.

5. Our investigations indicate the greater probability of a future decline in the U.S. home construction.

6. Numerical results are presented as a demonstration of the efficiency of the algorithms from two points of view: mesh quality and computational effort.

7. Results show the higher R-value of transparent composites panels over that of current glazing systems.

8. I argue in favor of a constructivist theory of truth in opposition to other theories.

As you probably noticed, the *that* clause variants give a somewhat greater emphasis to the findings than their noun-phrase equivalents.

Before we look at the abstract moves that deal with conclusions, let us briefly consider some more data from Hyland, this time from eight fields (Hyland, 2004).

**Table 2: Percentage of Abstracts Containing Particular Moves
(rounded percentages)**

	1980	1997
1. Introduction/background	33	47
2. Purpose/objective	72	81
3. Method	48	49
4. Product/results	96	95
5. Conclusion/implications/discussion/significance	7	22

The table shows that Move 4 in RA abstracts remains almost universal. Percentages for Move 3 (method) also changed very little, regularly appearing in some fields, but rarely in others. In contrast, major increases between 1980 and 1997 occurred in the opening and closing moves. Hyland ascribes these to increasing competition to get papers accepted by journals and to increasing competition to subsequently attract readers. As a result, the introduction in an abstract can function to promote the importance of the topic, while the conclusion can emphasize the significance of the study. Participants in our workshops and classes have also pointed out that these changes may partly be the result of increasingly strict journal requirements.

This data shows that even by 1997 distinctive and evaluative conclusions were quite rare in RA abstracts across the wide range of disciplines investigated. However, it is widely believed that in the biomedical field and in technological fields such as engineering and computer science there are often greater efforts to "boost" or promote the significance of the results. Huckin (2001), for example, found that 78 percent of his 90 biomedical abstracts had a conclusion move (5).

Concluding a Traditional Abstract (Move 5)

To check on this, we studied 25 abstracts from the 2006 issues of *Computer Modeling in Engineering and Science* (CMES), a field where promotional elements might be expected. At least 18 of the 25 (72 percent) appeared to have definite and upbeat conclusions, often stressing the utility or applicability of the reported results. Here are some examples (often in skeletal form) (our emphases):

1. We . . . conclude that *the new methods can be applied to* the calculation of large rotations.

2. The general characteristics . . . *demonstrate the capability* of the proposed procedure for locating sources of . . .

3. The algorithm developed by . . . is found to *be a robust, fast and efficient method* for detecting . . .

4. Some numerical examples are given *to demonstrate the power and scope of the method.*

5. *The accuracy and efficiency of* . . . approach *was verified* by analyzing the . . .

6. Through the simulations, *it is clearly demonstrated* that MATES is *a powerful tool* to study complex city traffic problems precisely.

Here it is worth noting that the majority of these 25 papers originated in Asian countries. Even so, the authors had little hesitation in concluding that their work is of relevance and importance. This finding contradicts a widely held belief that it is primarily Americans who use this kind of self-promotion. Rather, it would seem that an international disciplinary consensus has emerged, even if it might have originally been a result of U.S. influence. However, we need to point out that these findings come from a single journal.

Task Nine

A. We have suggested that the extracts from the CMES abstracts are clearly evaluative. Here are four less certain final sentences from the abstracts. Decide whether in your opinion they are descriptive (D) or (positively) evaluative (E).

   1. _____ Selected numerical results are presented to demonstrate the effect of non-homogeneity on dynamic response of the media.

   2. _____ It is also clarified that the penetration takes place from the inter-space of the network.

   3. _____ The J-R curves obtained also qualitatively agree with those of experiments, and the fracture surface is well simulated.

   4. _____ The number of cracks was correctly estimated, even when the plural cracks were closely located and the measured electrical potential distribution was similar to that of a single crack.

B. Examine the final sentences from the reference collection of RAs from your own field. What similarities and differences do you find between the CMES abstracts and those from your own area? Do you have any explanation for the differences? In particular, look for *strength of claim*.

C. Sometimes RA abstracts end with *general implications*. Here are two examples.

   1. Overall, these findings suggest that the government needs to reconsider certain aspects of its low-income housing policy.

   2. The research reported in this paper indicates that the survival of this species may be threatened.

   Do you find this kind of conclusion in your abstract sample? Are the conclusions hedged, as with *suggest* and *may be* in Task Nine? And do you find even more vague endings such as, *The implications of the study are discussed?*

D. In some fields, RA abstracts also end with recommendations as in:

   More attention needs to be given to early diagnosis of the disease.

   Recommendations are made regarding language training for future research, as well as suggestions for future research.

   Do recommendations occur as Move 5 in your mini-corpus?

Finally, note that a concluding statement (Move 5) contains the last words that a reader will read in the abstract. Obviously, in this context, it is better to try and say something meaningful—something to which the reader can attach significance.

A Final Issue: A Need to Problematize in the Abstract?

Academics are famous for problematizing. We often attempt to show that matters are not so clear, nor so simple, nor so unimportant as generally thought. We often do this in order to justify or prepare the way for our own research. Some of the abstracts or part-abstracts we have dealt with offer some problematizing as part of their background statements but some do not.

Task Ten

Here are some background statements from material that we have already seen (often in skeletal form).
   Do they

   A. directly problematize?

   B. indirectly problematize?

   C. not problematize at all?

1. _____ . . . programs are expanding rapidly but evidence of their effects is unknown.

2. _____ The . . . formation of cracks in biscuits . . . is an issue that manufacturers would like to predict and avoid.

3. _____ The purpose of this study . . . was to identify risk factors . . . .

4. _____ Many scholars claim that democracy improves the welfare of the poor.

5. _____ As yet little is known about the . . . characteristics of today's undergraduate students.

6. _____ Increasing globalization is thought to be impacting business communications around the world.

We have now worked through all the material designed to help you to construct a proficient traditional abstract. It is now time to put all the analysis and all the discussion to the test.

Task Eleven

Draft an RA abstract based on some research project you are or recently have been engaged in or, if this is not possible, write an RA abstract for somebody else's research paper. If you find it difficult to get started, try identifying in the longer RA a sentence that could serve as a summary for each of the abstract moves. (This is sometimes known as *reverse-outlining*.)

As you construct the draft, consider this twelve-item checklist. Think about why you are making particular decisions. Do you need to change anything?

____ 1. My draft falls within the required word limit.

____ 2. My research is fairly typical of the subfield. (If not, please go to #11.)

____ 3. The number of sentences is appropriate.

____ 4. The draft has the expected number of moves.

____ 5. I have considered the pros and cons of an opening problematizing move.

____ 6. I have considered whether a purpose statement is necessary.

____ 7. I have made sure that the methods move is not too long.

____ 8. I have reviewed the main tense options of present (for Moves 1, 2, and 5) and past (Moves 3 and 4).

____ 9. The main findings are sufficiently highlighted.

____ 10. As for conclusions, I have followed typical practice in my subfield.

____ 11. Since my research is unusual, I have considered whether I need to justify the topic and/or the approach in the opening two moves.

____ 12. Throughout I have checked whether any acronyms or abbreviations will be understood.

Now consider this scenario. A visiting scholar in your institution is a Brazilian professor of Nursing with somewhat limited experience writing research English. She has written an article in Portuguese (with colleagues) on the dental health of adolescents in her home area. The Brazilian journal requires an abstract in English as well. You offer to edit her draft abstract.

Task Twelve

Think about the content—is there anything you think might be added? Also, consider the checklist in Task Eleven. Next edit the abstract for language.

The importance of buccal[a] health for adolescents of different social strata of Ribeirão Preto

Abstract

The objective of the present study is to know the importance of buccal health for adolescents of different social strata, identifying the importance of dental aesthetics, and the care that these students take in relation to their buccal health. The methodological process adopted in this investigation is of qualitative nature, using as technique of collection of data the semi-structured interview. We know the importance of buccal health in several contexts of their lives, as in their personal appearance, sexuality, employment, and general health. This investigation allows to know the motivations of adolescents to preserve their buccal health, and we believe to be so valid to develop health promotion through health education. (111 words)

Note
[a] a medical adjective, here referring to the mouth area

Structured Research Article Abstracts

In many ways, "structured" and "traditional" abstracts are very similar in their content, style, and organization. However, one obvious difference is that with the former, the moves are *explicitly labeled.* In this section, we deal with so-called structured abstracts—those with labeled sub-sections.

As previously noted, structured abstracts were first adopted around 1987 in medicine and have since spread to several other fields, particularly the biological sciences and some areas of psychology. In the summer of 2007, ERIC (the Educational Research Information Center), a very large U.S. bibliographic database, stated that in the future it would adopt the structured abstract format.

One scholar who has long investigated the advantages of structured abstracts is James Hartley, a British professor of psychology. In 2004, he published a review entitled "Current Findings from Research on Structured Abstracts." Here is his own structured abstract for that review article:

Background: Structured abstracts were introduced into medical research journals in the mid-1980s. Since then they have been widely used in this and other contexts.

Aim: The aim of this paper is to summarize the main findings from research on structured abstracts and to discuss the limitations of some aspects of this research.

Method: A narrative literature review of all the relevant papers known to the author was conducted.

Results: Structured abstracts are typically longer than traditional ones, but they are also judged to be more informative and accessible. Authors and readers also judge them to be more useful than traditional abstracts. However, not all studies use "real-life" published examples from different authors in their work, and more work needs to be done in some cases.

Conclusions: The findings generally support the notion that structured abstracts can be profitably introduced into research journals. Some arguments for this, however, have more support than others.

Task Thirteen

Consider and, if appropriate, discuss these questions.

1. What are advantages of using structured abstracts, and what potential problems can be associated with their use?

2. The research suggests that structured abstracts are easier to read, but much of this research has used undergraduate students as subjects. Would the same conclusions be found with more senior researchers?

3. As Hartley notes, structured abstracts tend to be longer; his own is 153 words. Journals published by Emerald now require structured abstracts for all the articles and Emerald states that "abstracts should contain no more than 250 words." Do you find the Hartley abstract a little repetitive? And if so, does this matter?

4. Should authors be able to choose their own section titles, or should a journal have a standard set? (For example, *Aim* is sometimes called *Objective* or *Purpose*.)

5. Hartley argues that the five-move labeling can also apply to survey or review articles such as his own. In this context, what do you think about his own Method section?

6. Why are structured abstracts apparently more widely used in some fields rather than in others?

Statements of Objective

Task Fourteen

Below are twelve sample part concordance lines[6] from our corpus of structured Perinatology RA abstracts. All the extracts *immediately* follow the all–upper case heading OBJECTIVE; in other words, they represent part of the opening sentence of the Objective section. Scan the lines, and do the tasks that follow.

OBJECTIVE:

1. To determine whether there is an unconfounded association between. . . .
2. The purpose of this study was to evaluate how this change affected the rate of. . . .
3. To examine maternal and neonatal outcomes in expectant management of. . . .
4. To compare immediate changes in lung compliance following the administration of. . . .
5. This study was conducted to examine the relation between iron status and. . . .
6. To determine whether apnea in preterm infants is associated with. . . .
7. The optimal method of epinephrine administration during . . . is not known.
8. To evaluate the impact of birth weight on development of. . . .
9. Despite the high frequency of . . . , there has been no previous investigation . . . to. . . .
10. The epidemiology of . . . in developing countries has been poorly studied.
11. Prospectively validate an antenatal . . . risk score . . . at two public health . . . clinics.
12. The aim of this cohort, prospective study was to compare the diagnostic value of. . . .

---

[6] A *corpus* is a collection of texts or transcripts, increasingly today in electronic form for ease of manipulation. A *concordance* is a list of all occurrences of a keyword or phrase in a corpus—in this case, expressions following the word *Objective*.

1. Which of these do you consider not to be concerned with Objective? (In these cases, we do not wish to imply, however, that the sentence following might not describe the purpose.)

2. Of the "true" objective/purpose statements, how many begin directly with a *to* + VERB formulation? What are the advantages and disadvantages of this formulation?

3. How do you interpret Objective 11?

4. Four "purposive" verbs were used twice: *compare, determine, evaluate,* and *examine.* Would these be common Objective verbs in your field? If not, what words might you find?

Task Fifteen

The structured abstract from a 2007 article by G. D. Carnegie and S. P. Walker entitled "Household Accounting in Australia: Prescription and Practice from the 1820s to the 1960s" follows. Read the abstract, and answer the questions.

Abstract

Purpose—Beyond the public world of work, the home provides an arena[a] for examining accounting and gender in everyday life. This study aims to examine household accounting in Australia from the early nineteenth to around the mid-twentieth century.

Design/methodology/approach—The study comprises two parts. The first part, as reported in this paper, presents evidence on household accounting as prescribed in the didactic literature[b] in Australia, and evidence of actual accounting practices based on the examination of 76 sets of surviving Australian household records available in public repositories.[c] The second part adopts a microhistorical approach involving the detailed scrutiny[d] of 18 sets of accounting records and relevant biographical and family data on the household accountants involved.

Findings—The study indicates that household accounting was an instrument for restraining female consumption,[e] particularly during times of crises, and that accounting in Australian homes focused on maintaining records of routine transactions as opposed to the preparation of budgets and financial statements. Household accounting in Australia was performed by women and men. The surviving records examined suggest that while areas of financial responsibility were defined by gender there was little evidence of formalized hierarchical accountability[f] between spouses as has been found to be the case in Britain.

Originality/value—The study extends knowledge of household accounting and gender. Most historical investigations on this subject draw on instructional literature. The current investigation also examines accounting practice in the home.

Keywords: Accounting, Accounting history, Accounts, Australia
Article Type: General review
103 References
Article URL: http://www.emeraldinsight.com/10.1108/09513570710731209

Notes
[a] site, location
[b] educational literature, manuals of helpful hints
[c] libraries, archives, etc.
[d] close examination
[e] expenditure, spending money
[f] the husband controls the finances

1. How does the abstract reflect the *Prescription and Practice* subtitle?

2. Sentence 2 of the Design section includes the clause *as reported in this paper.* Is this necessary? Can you imagine why it might be included?

3. What kinds of "crises" are likely being referred to in the Findings section?

4. This is an RA abstract published in an Emerald journal, and at 233 words, it is under the 250-word limit. Emerald states on its website that four fields are obligatory:

    1. Purpose

    2. Design/methodology/approach

    3. Findings

    4. Originality/value

The site also says that there are two optional elements that may be included if applicable and placed between 3 and 4:

- Research limitations/implications
- Practical implications

Now draft an extra section/move/field to include either of these. Be imaginative!

Task Sixteen

Convert the political science abstract used in Task Two (page 3) into a structured abstract. Be prepared to discuss any difficulties you encountered. Alternatively, convert the abstract you wrote for Task Eleven (page 24) into a structured format.

Language Focus: Opening the Conclusion Section

As we have seen, in structured abstracts, the final section (Move 5) is typically labeled *Conclusion* or *Conclusions.*

Two questions arise:

1. Do we jump right in with, say, *Vitamin C does not prevent colds,* or do we start with sentence initial formulaic expressions such as these?

   - *The present findings provide further evidence that* Vitamin C does not prevent colds.
   - *These data show that* Vitamin C does not prevent colds.

2. For the main statements in a conclusion, do we use the present or past tense? Is this a free choice, or is it determined by the content?

First, to Question 1: An analysis of 60 opening Conclusion sentences from *structured* abstracts in the Perinatology corpus showed that only eight used a reporting verb formula.

Four of these were hedged or weakened, as in:

These preliminary results suggest that . . . .

Clearly then, the authors of these papers wished to make it clear that they were somewhat cautious about the conclusions they could draw.

Three other papers used this structure in the opposite way—to strengthen their claim:

The present findings *provide further evidence of . . . .*

Our findings clearly demonstrated that . . . .

The remaining instance was, in effect, neutral and so added little to the sentence and might thus have been omitted:

These data indicate that. . . .

Conclusion/Recommendation (!): In conclusions to a structured abstract, opt for a reporting verb formula if you feel the need to stress either the *strength* or the *weakness* of the main conclusion.

Now to Question 2, which deals with the tense used in Conclusion sections.

In the Perinatology corpus, there was a very strong preference (53 out of 60 tokens) for the present tense, presumably to show that the findings have contemporary relevance. Just ten of these main statements were modified by a modal verb or by a hedging verb phrase, such as *appears to be*. (There was also a single instance of *should*, which was—as might be imagined—a recommendation.)

So are there cases among the seven past instances when the past would seem to be required? Consider:

1. Outcome *was* favorable in 85% of IVM cases, . . .

Here the present would seem odd because the statement refers to the *cases examined by these particular researchers.*

2. A simple prediction-scoring model for LNS *was* developed.

Again the present tense would seem odd. After all, this conclusion is, in effect, a summary of what was done.

In other cases, the matter seems to be one of personal choice, although in this particular corpus, authors seem to want to opt for the present wherever possible.

Task Seventeen

Re-examine your collection of 10–15 abstracts from your target journals (structured or traditional). Find the statements that seem to introduce Conclusion/ Discussion/Significance. Examine the abstracts in terms of Question 2 on page 32. Be prepared to report your findings.

Abstracts for Short Communications

In addition to research articles, some research journals also include a number of shorter pieces. These go by a variety of names and titles, such as *short communications, scientific letters, technical notes, research notes,* and *case studies.* Some (but not all) of these shorter pieces have abstracts, which, in these cases, are sometimes called *summaries.* In some instances, these abstracts are about as long as those for full articles (say 100–150 words); in these cases, they follow the patterns previously outlined. On other occasions, they are shorter. It is this second shorter kind that is the subject of this section.

Here is a first example from a five-page *research note* (sentence numbers have been added).

Antiracist/multicultural teacher education: A focus on student teachers

Abstract: ①A survey of 221 students graduating from the teacher education program at the University of Manitoba, Canada reveals student attitudes regarding equity, diversity and multiculturalism in Canada and the roles and responsibilities of public schools in a multicultural society. ② Conflicting student responses suggest the need for a more detailed exploration of student perspectives toward antiracist education.[a]

Note
[a] educational attempt to develop greater understanding and tolerance of ethnic differences

Although this abstract has as many as 56 words, it contains just two sentences.

- Sentence 1 combines a Method Move (3) *(A survey of . . .)* with a Results Move (4) *(reveals student attitudes . . .).*
- Sentence 2 offers one implication of the findings (Move 5).

Task Eighteen

Can you now analyze these three abstracts in terms of their moves? (Sample answers for the tasks can be found in the *Commentary* at www.press. umich.edu/esl/compsite/ETRW/.)

1. A 2004 four-page *letter* from an ornithology journal

The occurrence of owls in the Marshall Islands

Abstract:

①Short-eared owls *(Asio flammeus)* are capable of crossing long stretches of open water and have been successful colonizers of islands. ② In the central and western Pacific two established populations (on Hawai'i and on Pohnpei in Micronesia) seem to be the foci of repeated dispersal events. ③ The paper reviews the historic and linguistic record for the occurrence of short-eared owls on the scattered atolls of the Marshall Islands, the easternmost group of Micronesia.

2. A 1997 working paper *case study*

Consolidation on the medical care marketplace: A case study from Massachusetts

Abstract:

① This paper examines consolidation in the Massachusetts hospital market. ② We find that consolidation is driven primarily by a large decline in the demand for hospital beds, resulting from increased enrollment in managed care and technological changes. ③ The drive to consolidate appears through three primary forces: consolidation for closure; consolidation for economies of scale; and consolidation for network creation.

3. Opening entry to a 2005 *Forum* discussion

Collision rules for high-speed craft

Abstract:

① Re-visiting the requirement to introduce amended collision regulations to meet the developing threat in encounters between high-speed craft and slower, mainly smaller vessels. ② This paper looks at the requirements of different types of encounter and the ability to identify high-speed craft through AIS.[a] ③ It introduces proposed changes to the Colregs that could help to reduce the threat to small, slow craft.

Note
[a] Automatic Identification System

Task Nineteen

Here we offer a one-page piece from the December 23, 1995, issue of the *British Medical Journal*. This short communication is not long, and we think you will enjoy reading it! (We have also provided a few explanatory notes.) The original did not have an abstract or summary. After reading it, construct a suitable short communication abstract for the paper. Aim for an abstract of between 60 and 80 words.

Why do old men have big ears?

James A. Heathcote

In July 1993, 19 members of the south east Thames faculty of the Royal College of General Practitioners gathered at Bore Place,[a] in Kent, to consider how best to encourage ordinary general practitioners to carry out research. Some members favoured highly structured research projects, others were fired by serendipity[b] and the observations of everyday practice. Someone said, "Why do old men have big ears?" Some members thought this was obviously true—indeed some men have very big ears—but others doubted it, and so we set out to answer the question "As you get older do your ears get bigger?"

Methods and results

Four ordinary general practitioners agreed to ask patients attending routine surgery[c] consultations for permission to measure the size of their ears, with an explanation of the idea behind the project. The aim was to ask consecutive patients aged 30 or over, of either sex, and of any racial group. Inevitably it was sometimes not appropriate—for example, after a bereavement[d] or important diagnosis—to make what could have seemed so frivolous[e] a request, and sometimes (such as when a surgery was running late) patients were not recruited. The length of the external ear was measured from the top to the lowest part with a transparent ruler; the result (in millimetres), together with the patient's age, was recorded. No patient refused to participate, and all the researchers were surprised by how interested (if amused) patients were by the project. The data were then entered on to a computer and analysed with Epi-Info[f]; the relation between length of ear and the patient's age was examined by calculating a regression equation. In all, 206 patients were studied (mean age 53.75 (range 30–93); median age 53 years). The mean ear length was 67.5 mm (range 52.0–84.0 mm), and the linear regression equation was: ear length = 55.9 + (0.22 x patient's age) (95% confidence intervals for B coefficient 0.17 to 0.27). The figure shows a scatter plot of the relation between length of ear and range.

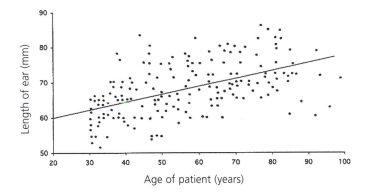

It seems therefore that as we get older our ears get bigger (on average by 0.22 mm a year).

Comment

A literature search on Medline[g] by the library at the Royal college of General Practitioners that looked for combinations of "ears, external," "size and growth," "males," and "aging" produced no references.

A chance observation—that older people have bigger ears—was at first controversial but has since been shown to be true. For the researchers, the experience of involving patients in business beyond their presenting symptoms proved to be a positive one, and it was rewarding to find a clear result. Why ears should get bigger when the rest of the body stops growing is not answered by this research. Nor did we consider whether this change in a particular part of the anatomy is a marker of something less easily measurable elsewhere or throughout the body.

I acknowledge the generous help of Drs Colin Smith and David Armstrong and Ms Sandra Johnston with the data analysis; the work of my fellow data collectors, Drs Ian Brooman, Keren Hull, and David Roche; and the support of all members of the Bore Place group.

<u>Notes</u>
[a] a conference and study center in the countryside south east of London. In this piece, the original British spellings have been retained throughout.
[b] inspired by lucky chances or lucky breaks
[c] the British term for a doctor's office hours or appointments; it has nothing to do with surgical operations
[d] grief following the death of somebody close
[e] unnecessarily light-hearted or silly
[f] a software program for epidemiologists, public health and medical professionals used for entering and analyzing data
[g] The U.S. national Library of Medicine's search service

Task Twenty

Now compare your abstract with these four written by participants in our classes (with some minor editing). What are the strengths and weaknesses of each? If you like, begin by ranking them from best to worst.

A. ① This paper investigates a seemingly-obvious, but still interesting question "As you get older, do your ears get bigger?" ② From the measurement data of ear size across people of various racial groups and ages and following linear regression results, we find that there is a statistically significant correlation between age and ear size. ③ The reason behind this finding is not addressed in this paper nor in previous studies, and needs further research. (71 words)

B. ① In a chance experiment inspired by the question "why do old men have big ears?" four general practitioners asked patients attending for routine surgery consultation permission to measure the size of their ears. ② Analyzed data from 206 patients show that as we get older, our ears get bigger by about 0.22 mm per year. ③ Our research does not explain the cause of this growth. ④ The experiment, however, was rewarding. (69 words)

C. ① The relationship between ear size and age has been one of the most interesting questions among general practitioners from the early 1990s. ② To verify a hypothesis that one's ears get bigger as one gets older, a regression equation of patients' ages and ear sizes has been obtained by direct measurements and statistical analysis. ③ The result shows that the ear size increases as time progresses, and the average increase is 0.22 mm a year. ④ In the present research, the relationship between ear size and age has been revealed for the first time. (91 words)

D. ① This short paper reports on a study measuring the size of ears against age. ② Involving 206 human subjects, it documents ear size and age. ③ Epi-Info analysis and a regression equation show that, with a 5% chance of error, people's ears get bigger by .22 mm a year. ④ Yet, as to why ears keep growing while the rest of the body does not, this study has not come to an answer. (70 words)

Task Twenty-One

The draft title and abstract of a case study we are working on follows. The editor has told us to reduce the abstract to 75 words maximum.
What deletions or other editing would you suggest?

Writing for publication:
A case study of a seminar series for post-docs in Perinatology

Abstract:

① We were approached in 2005 by the Perinatalogy Research Branch (PRB) of the U.S. Government to help its post-doctoral fellows (N = 35–40) with writing up their research for publication. ② In 2006 we ran a series of five six-hour seminars. ③ Specialized materials were developed including the construction of a specialized electronic corpus of 120 perinatal research articles. ④ The basic principle of the materials was to develop participants' (both international and U.S.) sense of the discoursal world of research in which they had specialized via textual explorations and tasks of various kinds. ⑤ Evaluations were positive, although the number of attendees was sometimes disappointing. ⑥ Suggestions are made for a revised program to be run in the future. (115 words)

Conference Abstracts

Hofstadter's Law (1979) states that:

> *It always takes longer than you expect, even when you take Hofstadter's Law into account.*

The next genre we deal with is the conference abstract (CA). We consider this to be a different genre because both its context and its purpose are very different to those of a journal abstract. In terms of context, CAs are independent, free-standing texts that succeed or fail on their own merits. Another way we can see that the CA is a different genre arises from the fact that the CA has its own title, while a journal abstract is usually simply headed by *Abstract* or indeed may have no heading at all. As for purpose, CAs are texts designed to get their authors onto conference programs. The goal then in writing a CA is to impress the conference proposal reviewers, who in fact may have little time to read and assess your proposal. Given the purpose in writing and submitting a CA is to create an opportunity to present your work, your CA will typically be somewhat promotional; in effect, it will typically attempt to "sell" your work.

As previously mentioned, the majority of CAs are "unstructured" (i.e., continuous text), sometimes divided into paragraphs. However, in certain medical specialties at least, sectioned or "structured" conference abstracts are increasingly being adopted. We deal with the traditional CA first because it is still much more widespread.

Task Twenty-Two

Consider these questions, and answer them as best you can for your area of study. Please compare your answers with some of those provided by participants in our courses. (Sample answers for the tasks can be found in the *Commentary* at www.press.umich.edu/esl/compsite/ETRW/.) Be prepared to discuss your findings.

1. The CA typically has to be submitted months ahead of the actual conference. How far in advance—in months—of a conference are CAs usually submitted in your field?

2. Some small regional or local conferences may accept nearly all the CAs received; major national or international ones may reject up to 75 percent of the CAs. What are typical acceptance rates for conferences in your field?

3. The CA is a freestanding (and often anonymous) document that has to impress a review committee. Are CAs in your field blind reviewed? That is, does the review committee select papers without seeing the names of the authors (and their institutional affiliations)?

4. Conference abstracts often have rigorous word or space limits, and the number of words allowed never seems to be quite enough! What are the typical word limits in your field?

5. Most CAs need to create a research space for themselves prior to reporting the actual findings. As a result, the first half of a CA may be devoted to "justifying the topic." Would this be true of your field?

6. Because the CA is a challenging and complex promotional genre, it usually requires several drafts. If you can arrange it, input from colleagues and friends can be quite helpful. Who could you (or would you) turn to for help?

A Closer Look at the Organization of Conference Abstracts

Recent studies of unstructured conference abstracts suggest the following six-part organization, although some CAs will not have all the parts, or moves:

Move 1: Outlining/promoting/problematizing the research field or topic

Move 2: Justifying this particular piece of research/study

Move 3: Methodological, demographic, or procedural comments

Move 4: Summarizing the main findings

Move 5: Highlighting its outcome/results

Move 6: Further observations (implications, limitations, future developments)

The extra move comes about because many conference abstracts need to make a strong appeal to the review committees.

Task Twenty-Three

Read this abstract, and answer the questions that follow. It was submitted to a mid-size Information Science conference by a doctoral student in one of our classes.

Collaboratory use and social network change in the space science community

Abstract

① While collaboration has always played an important role in scientific research, information technology has introduced new opportunities for collaborative research. ② In particular, collaboratories, which use computer networks to facilitate scientists' access to remote instruments, to remote colleagues, and to archived data, represent a novel environment for scientific collaboration. ③ By diminishing the importance of physical proximity, collaboratories provide a technological basis for new forms of networks of scholars (Wellman, 2002). ④ Based on previous studies of information technology use and on the social networks of scientists, it is here hypothesized that collaboratory use may extend network range. ⑤ One likely pathway for this is by generating more opportunities for junior scientists and those employed by non-doctoral institutions to become inter-connected in ways comparable to the networks of senior scientists at elite institutions. ⑥ On the basis of a survey of space scientists and on an examination of co-authorship relations among those scientists from 1993 to 1996, this longitudinal study compares space scientists' social network structure before and after they adopted the *Upper Atmospheric Research Collaboratory* in order to examine its impact on their scientific work. ⑦ Results of this research indicate that collaboratory use has led to an increase in the network range of the aerospace science community. ⑧ More specifically, junior scientists and peripheral institutes have become more connected to senior scientists and elite institutes. ⑨ The paper closes by discussing whether the space science collaboratory is typical of others or has distinctively predisposing collaborative features.

—(Airong Luo—minor editing)

Part A: Evaluation

Do you agree (✓) or disagree (X) with the following comments made by participants in a workshop? (For Comments 4 and 5, remember that in many fields it
is typically more prestigious for an abstract to be accepted for a presentation
rather than for a poster session.)

1. _____ "It tells a good story, and one that is easy to follow. There's no ambi-
guity or confusion here."

2. _____ "The relevance of the study is well established, but the actual results
are rather vague. I suspect the author has collected the data but not
yet really analyzed it."

3. _____ "References are thin; there are no references to previous work on
scientists' social networks, and none to this particular collaboratory!"

4. _____ "I vote to accept it as a presented paper."

5. _____ "I recommend accepting it only as a poster presentation."

Part B. Analysis

The nine-sentence abstract has a typical shape. The content narrows as it moves
from background to topic to results, but then it widens out in the final sentence. This shape is illustrated in Figure 3.

Figure 3. Shape of Task Twenty-Three CA

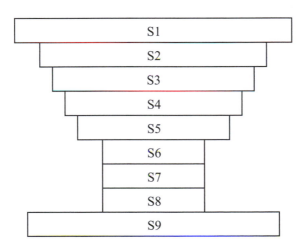

1. Here is the first part of a "move analysis." Complete the second half (noting that not all moves may be realized). If a move is not present, mark the move as NA (not applicable).

    Move 1   (Background/introduction/problematization) *Sentences 1–3*

    Move 2   (Present research/purpose) *Sentences 4–5*

    Move 3   (Methods/materials/procedures)

    Move 4   (Results/findings)

    Move 5   (Highlighting the results)

    Move 6   (Implications/imitations, etc.)

2. Is *collaboratory* sufficiently defined in Sentence 2?

3. Which sentence has the most hedging, and why?

4. Are the results given in a general to specific order, or the reverse?

5. What examples of promotional language can you find? Where do they mainly occur? What is the most common promotional claim made in this case? What others might be made?

6. As is typical, in the second half there are some metadiscoursal elements such as:

    Sentence 6. This longitudinal study compares . . .

    Sentence 7. Results of this research indicate that . . .

    Sentence 9. The paper closes by . . .

    Could the author have written any of these instead?

    Sentence 6. The longitudinal study compares . . .

    Sentence 7. The research results indicate that . . .

    Sentence 9. This paper closes by . . .

7. What, in your opinion, is the effect on the reader of the nice phrase in S9, *The paper closes by . . . ?*

8. In this regard, how do you react to the following commentary on *this* by Finnish discourse analyst Anna Mauranen (1993)?

    One rhetorical effect that *this* produces is an impression of closeness and solidarity between reader and writer. It has the effect of bringing the reader round to the writer's orientation, or point of view, by implying that the writer as well as the reader are both "here," on the same side, looking at things from the same perspective.

Task Twenty-Four

Study a couple of conference abstracts from your field (your own and/or borrowed examples from colleagues, advisors, or instructors or found on the Internet). How are they similar to and different from the six-move model we have offered? What explanations might you have for any differences that you find?

One of the points we have been emphasizing in CAs is the need for a solid introductory section that motivates your study and will likely attract the attention of the selection committee. Often this involves some opening background information; this is then followed by some kind of problematization, such as revealing a gap in current knowledge (Moves 1 and 2). Mature CAs of this type often have "the shape" illustrated in Figure 3. To check your capacity to recognize this, you may like to spend a little time on the following task.

Task Twenty-Five

A longer conference abstract from a technical field follows. However, the seven sections are not in the right order. Can you re-arrange them and put them in the original order? Work with a partner if possible. Remember the move structure we have been discussing.

Transparent façade panel typologies based on hybrid bio-composite and recyclable polymer materials

A. Our research program includes the design and development of prototype panel systems, the evaluation of structural and thermal performance, together with their role in reducing energy consumption and pollution emission through life cycle analysis.

B. It is essential that we find ways to save on energy consumption through the use of solar energy, improved thermal insulation, and alternative efficient glazed façade systems. In this paper, we demonstrate how alternative typologies of transparent and translucent load-bearing façade systems based on biocomposite and recyclable materials, are structurally and thermally efficient at the same time they contribute towards reduced pollutant emissions and non-renewable material uses.

C. Buildings are large consumers of energy. In the United States of America, they constitute over 33% of the total annual energy consumption, produce 35% of the total carbon dioxide emissions and attribute 40% of landfill wastes. The building industry is also a large consumer of non-renewable materials and this trend has escalated dramatically over the past century.

D. The materials are configured to work as composite panels systems made from a combination of bio-composite and recyclable polymer materials. These materials are environmentally sustainable, because they either originate from naturally grown renewable resources or are recyclable.

E. The paper also discusses the fundamentals of the research investigations and predicts good energy efficiency, making the product a sustainable alternative when used in building applications. The paper highlights areas of ongoing research and applications by hybrid composite façade systems, which will make the approach a viable option for the building industry, in the future.

F. Composite insulated panel systems are used extensively in the engineering and building industry, owing to their structural and thermal efficiency. However, these systems are generally opaque and offer little flexibility in building applications. As an alternative, we demonstrate how building products comprised of hybrid material typologies can be made to perform efficiently as load-bearing façade systems that substitute for current glazing systems with adequate thermal and structural performance, which also possess good light transmission characteristics and integral shading capability.

G. The paper describes relevant applications and related current research activities, being carried out by the authors, under an EPA/NSF funded grant project, titled People, Prosperity and Planet, in relation to prototypical composite panel systems. Our current area of investigation relates to typologies that use thermoplastic polymers (as skin material) and biocomposites (as a core material). Our evaluations have demonstrated viable applications and improved performance compared to conventional single and double glazing systems in buildings.

The Rating of Conference Abstracts

Of course, finding an appropriate structure for your conference abstract and providing a suitable scene setting are only part of the story. There are additionally the matters of offering "interestingness" and of projecting a convincing and authoritative image—of "positioning" yourself as a member of the disciplinary community. Berkenkotter and Huckin (1995) examined the properties of high-rated and low-rated abstracts submitted to a large humanities conference in the United States—the *Conference on College Composition and Communication*. Table 3 summarizes what they found.

Table 3: Abstract Descriptors

High-Rated Abstracts	Low-Rated Abstracts
Topics were of current interest to experienced members of the community.	Topics were of lesser interest.
A problem was clearly defined.	No clear problem was defined.
Problem was addressed in a novel way.	Problem, if defined, received less interesting treatment.
Special terminology was current, or "buzzy."[1]	Terminology was standard.
Several explicit and implicit references to the scholarly literature.	Fewer citations and allusions were used.

Source: Berkenkotter & Huckin (1995)

Of course, and as Berkenkotter and Huckin (1995) readily concede, each field will have its own perceptions as to what makes a conference abstract a "winning" one. Certainly, other fields, perhaps especially in science, may not associate "interestingness" so closely with novelty. Rather, they may value the cumulative addition of a new piece of evidence, such as a piece of research that confirms or updates previous findings.

---

[1] *Buzzwords* are those of great topical interest; at the time of writing these would include *sustainability, green,* and anything beginning with *nano.*

Task Twenty-Six

Assume that you have been appointed as a member of the review committee for a conference in your field. You have been asked to make a ranked list of the qualities that the committee should be looking for in the abstracts that it accepts. Make that list. Here are four ranked lists of the top three criteria from our students. You may find them helpful as you think about this. Alternatively or in addition, you could check whether the major conference in your field gives proposal evaluation criteria on its website.

Mechanical Engineering	*Environmental Sciences*
1. Novelty, originality	1. Urgency of the problem
2. Applicability/industrial impact	2. Good supporting data
3. Completeness	3. Applicable to real world
Dentistry	*Linguistics*
1. Interesting topic	1. Interesting phenomenon
2. Design of the study	2. Effect on theory
3. Benefit to patients	3. Amount of data

The Role of a Senior Author: An Example

As English language instructors and researchers, Chris and John are probably capable, at least most of the time, of assessing whether a draft abstract in their own field is well constructed and has that elusive quality of "interestingness." However, when we review the drafts of our course participants from fields distant to our own, we are probably better at asking questions rather than providing solutions. Here is a case in point. Although the two texts below are now out of date in terms of content, their comparison remains very instructive.

Several years ago, John was helping an Iranian student in electrical engineering prepare a draft conference abstract for the major biennial conference on sensors. The abstract needed to be about 600 words long and be accompanied by a number of drawings. (These features seem quite typical for engineering.) The third draft of the opening paragraph is shown on the left.

Third Draft	Fourth Draft with Dr. Wise's Revision
① Present measurement and automated control systems need to have sensors with higher reliability and accuracy than is practical with discrete and isolated components. ② In addition, issues such as cost optimization of testing, packaging, and interfacing with higher level control systems have provided the motivations to change microsensors from "isolated components" to "integrated system elements." ③ This paper describes the design of an addressable VSLI smart sensor capable of handing up to eight sensors with 12 bit accuracy, introduces a custom designed bus, and describes a new method for data compensation.	① As integrated transducers are combined with increasing amounts of on-chip or in-module circuitry, where to partition the electronic system and how much electronics to include with the "sensor" become major issues. ② Integrated sensors, particularly those associated with automated manufacturing, are likely to evolve into smart peripherals, and the definition of appropriate sensor interface standards is currently the subject of three national committees. ③ This paper describes a possible organization for such devices and appropriate interface protocols. ④ The device described is addressable, programmable, self-testing, compatible with a bidirectional digital sensor bus, and offers 12-bit accuracy using internally-stored compensation coefficients. ⑤ The design is sufficiently flexible to allow upward-compatible sensor designs to be inserted in existing equipment without reprogramming the host system and will accommodate differing sensor features.

As you can see, the opening of the abstract draft on the left is rather flat. True, it identifies a need and goes on in Sentence 3 to offer a (partial) solution to this need, but it seems rather unimaginative and over-reliant on technical detail. However, this was the third draft and seemed about the best a "lab rat" and a "grammar rat" could do after working together. The whole draft abstract was submitted to the lab director and senior professor for editing, a professor incidentally widely admired for his technical writing. He offered minor edits for the rest of the abstract but totally rewrote the opening paragraph. Professor Kensall Wise's version is on the right.

Here are some of the changes between Draft 3 and 4. In terms of the likely effect on the audience, which do you consider the most important?

	Third Draft	Fourth Draft
1.	Set in the narrow world of the laboratory setting.	Confident and dynamic sweep across the field as a whole; for example, Sentence 1 talks about "major issues."
2.	Sentence 2 talks about "the motivations" for change.	Sentence 2 moves to the national scene by mentioning that the definition of standards "is currently the subject of three national committees."
3.	It ends with a description of the design.	It ends by adding that "the design is sufficiently flexible to allow . . . ".

The episode we have described had a happy ending. The abstract was one of the 64 accepted for the conference. In fact, at this particular conference it is the reviewers' custom to rank the submissions numerically. The fourth draft was placed third! (If further evidence is needed of its high quality).

This story has been included to emphasize that the experienced researcher in your area is the best person to anticipate how other experts will react to your draft. A nonexpert cannot offer this valuable perspective.

The Problem of Promissory Abstracts

Academics and researchers make plans for the future. Alas, we often promise more than we can deliver. When looking to the future, we tend to assume a perfect world, one without illness, loss of data or of funding, technical problems, and so on. In some fields, we may need to submit a CA to a conference with less of the work done than we anticipated as the deadline for submission approaches. We are now faced with writing a *promissory abstract,* that is, one that projects what will be done by the time the conference comes around in several months' time.

Task Twenty-Seven

Read this abstract, and answer the questions that follow.

The role of natural variation in changing amphibian[a] populations

① For more than a decade now, numerous researchers (e.g., Doyle, 2006; Lee, 2007) have noted serious declines in the populations of many of the nearly 5,000 species of amphibians. ② This reduction has caused concern because amphibians are generally regarded as sensitive indicators of the planet's overall health. ③ Although much recent research has pointed to habitat destruction, particularly the draining[b] of wetlands, as the cause of the declines, the declines and apparent extinctions are widely occurring in areas far removed from human populations, as in the case of the once abundant golden toad[c] in the cloud forests of Costa Rica.

④ In order to provide a better understanding of the dwindling[d] amphibian population, my research will investigate whether the declines and extinctions are in fact indicative of a worldwide environmental crisis. ⑤ Analyzing data from as far back as the 1700s, I will show that amphibian populations are subject to year-to-year natural environmental variations, such as droughts and floods, that can affect egg laying and larvae survival and that much of the decline may in fact have less to do with human intrusion. ⑥ Along this same vein,[e] I will also investigate whether reports of increasing numbers of abnormalities in amphibians, such as missing eyes and limbs, can also be partly explained by natural environmental changes.

Notes
[a] frogs, toads, and salamanders
[b] the removal of water
[c] an animal similar to a frog, but with rougher, drier skin. Toads live mostly on land.
[d] declining, shrinking
[e] continuing this same line of thinking

1. Do you think that the research described in the abstract has actually been done? What in the abstract might suggest to a reviewer that it has not actually been completed?

2. What, if any, changes could be made so that it appears that some of the work has been completed?

3. Do you have any experience with promissory abstracts? If you have written one, were you able to actually come through with what you promised? Are these kind of promissory abstracts often accepted into the conference program?

Task Twenty-Eight

Now write your own draft conference abstract of 200–300 words based on one of your own research interests. If the abstract is *promissory*, add a note to your instructor explaining that some of results may be more anticipated rather than real! If your field expects structured abstracts, have a look first at pages 60–62 before drafting.

Conference Abstract Titles

Given the word and space constraints for abstracts, the titles you choose for CAs can be important. Remember that the title is your first opportunity to attract the reader of the conference program to your session. But before you start working on the title, you first need to check the maximum number of characters or words permitted. Once this is done, also consider the possibility of title divided by a colon. The first part can be an attention-getter, and the second part can give some specific detail, as in:

> Winning Combinations: K–16 Partnerships in Florida

Your title can raise a question that your research will address, as shown in these examples:

> Specificity Revisited: How Far Should We Go Now?
> Genetics in Kidney Disease: How Much Do We Want to Know?

Titles with colons can also make reference to the methodology used in the research. Such titles are fairly common in medical journals. In fact, according to Hartley (2007), as of 2003, the *British Medical Journal* has required all titles to have a colon after which the methodology of the study is given:

> Anticonvulsant Drugs for Management of Pain: A Systematic Review
> Cardiovascular Protection and Blood Pressure Reduction: A Motor-Analysis

In the broad field of the medical and life sciences, a relatively recent trend has been titles in the form of declarative sentences, as in, "Dietary Genistein Generates Reduced Blood Pressure in Female Mice." While these sentence-type titles are still in a minority, they seem to be preferred when clear results (positive or negative) can be communicated (as indeed with the abstract in Task Thirty).

Task Twenty-Nine ▓▓▓▓▓▓▓▓▓▓▓▓▓▓▓▓▓▓▓▓▓▓▓▓▓▓▓▓▓▓▓▓▓

Here are ten titles and opening sentences of unedited draft CAs from international students or visiting scholars we have worked with. Choose the two that are closest to your own area. Decide in each of the two cases whether the title plus Sentence 1:

a. are basically okay as they are

b. need some minor editing

c. require some substantial work.

If you chose b. or c., draft some editing changes.

_____ 1. Marketing and Economic Development: One More Time

One of the problematic issues in macromarketing is the question of whether marketing is a consequence of economic development or if economic development is a consequence of marketing.

_____ 2. A Novel Target of Cancer Treatment

Currently, metastatic cancers remain incurable diseases.

_____ 3. Chemical Speciation of Thallium in Natural Waters Using Catio Exchange Resin

Thallium is a potential pollutant, which is more toxic than lead and mercury.

_____ 4. Low Temperature Polycrystalline Silicon Thin Film Transistors with In-situ Doped Source and Drain

We have fabricated novel polycrystalline silicon thin film transistors (poly-Si TFTs) employing in-situ doping process in order to implement poly-Si CMOS TFT technology.

_____ 5. The Worst Case Scenario Generator

In recent years, the auto industry has been focused on active safety systems, which can help the drivers to avoid traffic accidents.

_____ 6. How Asynchronous Learning Technologies May Expand the Need for Computer Skills Training of Education Majors

The Web has become one of the most informative and diversified educational tools available to university instructors.

_____ 7. Do the New Technologies Create New Opportunities for Performing Arts?

Brenda Laurel said in her book Computers as Theatre *(1991) that new media are dramatic because of the way they present information.*

_____ 8. "Hoabinhian" Lithic Assemblages from Lang Kamnan Cave, Western Thailand

The status of "hoabinhian" has long been questioned by archaeologists for several decades.

_____ 9. A Case Study of Agroecosystem Health in Honduras: Focusing on the Roles of Livestock in Agricultural Communities

Small scale livestock production in the Tascalapa watershed of Honduras is an important method in which semi-subsistence farmers secure their livelihoods.

_____ 10. Analysis of Socio-cultural Influences on Japanese Families and the Social Welfare Policies in the Future

This paper examines the following questions: what has influenced and will influence the cultural norms in Japanese families; how they have developed and will develop; and how will current social welfare policies in the U.S. and Japan need to be adjusted in order to accommodate with the transitions in social circumstances of Japanese and other families?

Structured Conference Abstracts

We close this section with a brief look at structured conference abstracts. As far as we know, up until now these are mainly used in certain medical conferences, such as The Society of Thoracic Surgeons 2004 annual meeting (which Chris attended). Indeed, the structured CAs that have been accepted are apparently reproduced verbatim in the program. Here is an example.

Task Thirty

Read the abstract, and answer the questions that follow. A few explanatory notes follow the passage.

Sleep deprivation does not affect operative results in cardiac surgery

Background: (1) There has been an increasing trend towards the mandatory[a] reduction in work hours for physicians due to the fear that sleep deprived physicians are prone[b] to making mistakes. (2) We hypothesized that sleep deprivation would not be associated with increased morbidity [c] or mortality in cardiac operations.

Methods: (3) We retrospectively analyzed all cases performed by cardiac attending surgeons from January 1994 to April 2003. (4) Complication rates of cases performed by "sleep deprived" (SD) surgeons were compared with cases done when surgeons were "not sleep deprived" (NSD). (5) A surgeon was considered sleep deprived if he or she performed a case the night before that started between 10PM and 5AM, or ended between the hours of 11PM and 730AM.

Results: (6) A total of 6751 cases were recorded in the STS[d] database over the 9 year period examined. 339 of these cases (5%) were performed by SD surgeons, compared with 6412 (95%) of cases performed by NSD surgeons. (7) Mortality rates for CABG[e] operations showed no significant differences (1.7% (SD = 4/223) vs. 3.1% (NSD = 133/4206), $p = .34$). (8) A comparison of overall mortality rates ($p = .73$), as well as operative ($p = .46$), pulmonary[f] ($p = .60$), renal[g] ($p = .93$), neurologic

(p = .10), and infectious (p = .87) complications of all cases also failed to show any statistically significant differences between any group.

Conclusions: ⑨ Sleep deprivation does not affect operative morbidity or mortality in cardiac surgical operations.[2] These data do not support a need for work hour restrictions on cardiac surgeons.

Notes
[a] regulated or required by regulations or laws
[b] liable to or more likely to
[c] sickness or disease
[d] Society of Thoracic Surgeons database
[e] coronary bypass surgeries
[f] dealing with the lungs
[g] dealing with the kidneys

---

1. How do the authors highlight the importance of their work? Does it occur in the expected section?

2. Are you—or are you not—surprised by the way the hypothesis in Sentence 2 is formulated?

3. Do you think there is a good balance of information across the four named sections? Would you have liked more or less information in any of the four?

4. Notice that the authors of this abstract provide a definition of sleep deprivation in Sentence 5. Could the definition have occurred elsewhere? What do you think of this definition? When should definitions be used?

5. Some early research suggested that there was no space in abstracts for negative statements. So, what do you think about Sentences 7–10?

6. One possible advantage of structured abstracts of this sort is that it reduces the need for self-referring expressions such as, *The results show . . .* because the bolded section headings do this. Are there any disadvantages?

7. How would you describe the difference between Sentence 9 and Sentence 10?

8. How would you characterize the title of the abstract? Does this sort of title seem typical? What, if any, advantages might a title like this offer?

9. As it happens, Chris attended the conference at which this paper was given. How do you think the talk was received?

10. The abstract of the published paper is on page 62. What changes did the authors make? Do any of these seem significant?

Sleep deprivation does not affect
operative results in cardiac surgery

*Presented at the Fortieth Annual Meeting of The Society of
Thoracic Surgeons, San Antonio, TX, Jan 26–28, 2004*

Abstract

Background: There has been an increasing trend towards the mandatory reduction in work hours for physicians because of the fear that sleep-deprived (SD) surgeons are more prone to make mistakes. We hypothesized that sleep deprivation would not be associated with increased morbidity or mortality in cardiac operations.

Methods: A retrospective review was done of all cases performed by all attending cardiac surgeons from January 1994 to April 2003. Complication rates of cases performed by SD surgeons were compared with cases done when the surgeons were not sleep-deprived (NSD). A surgeon was deemed sleep deprived if he or she performed a case the previous evening that started between 10:00 PM and 5:00 AM, or ended between the hours of 11:00 PM and 7:30 AM.

Results: A total of 6,751 cases were recorded in the Society of Thoracic Surgeons database over the 9-year period examined. Of these, 339 cases (5%) were performed by SD surgeons, and 6,412 (95%) cases were performed by NSD surgeons. Mortality rates for coronary artery bypass operations showed no significant differences (1.7% [SD = 4/223] vs 3.1% [NSD = 133/4206)] p = 0.34). Operative (p = 0.47), pulmonary (p = 0.60), renal (p = 0.93), neurologic (p = 0.11), and infectious (p = 0.87) complications of all cases also failed to show any statistically significant differences in any group. Perfusion times, cross-clamp times, and the use of blood products were also similar between groups.

Conclusions: Sleep deprivation does not affect operative morbidity or mortality in cardiac surgical operations. These data do not support a need for work hour restrictions on surgeons.

Conference Program Abstracts or Summaries

After your proposal has (naturally!) been accepted, you may need to send a short summary to the conference organizers for inclusion in the conference booklet. Some conferences might even ask you to submit such summary together with your abstract. Here, you want to summarize the proposal in such a way that it attracts an audience of reasonable size.

The short program abstract may be your only opportunity to advertise your presentation to conference participants. Thus, you want to take a reasonable amount of time preparing it. The short abstract should say enough about your presentation so that the reader has a fairly good idea of what our talk wil be about.

Task Thirty-One

Here is a conference abstract (slightly modified) about conference abstracts! We follow it by three versions of a 50-word summary of the author's paper.

1. Can you identify the first, second, and third (final) drafts of the summary?

2. Which do you prefer?

Cultural variation in the genre of the conference abstract: Rhetorical and linguistic dimensions

Tatyana Yakhontova

① The conference abstract is a common and important genre that plays a significant role in distributing new knowledge within scientific communities, both national and international. ② As a genre with the specific features of "interestingness" created to attract the attention of reviewing committees, the conference abstract was first investigated by Berkenkotter & Huckin (1995) and Swales (1996). ③ However, the issue of cultural variation in the genre has not yet become a subject of research, although the conference abstract, like other genres of academic discourse, can be presumed to reflect national preferences in writing. ④ This paper attempts to describe the cultural-specific differences of

English versus Ukrainian and Russian conference abstracts on the level of their cognitive structure and language. ⑤ It also offers some tentative explanations of the cultural and ideological backgrounds underlying these rhetorical and textlinguistic preferences. ⑥ It will also be shown how the inherited cognitive patterns of Slavic writers interplay with the acquired stereotypes of English scientific discourse in the abstracts they construct in English. ⑦ These texts, hybrid from the viewpoint of their cultural shaping, can be regarded as evidence of the transition period typical of both sociopolitical and intellectual life of Ukraine and other states of the former Soviet Union. ⑧ As a result, this study raises a broader question: To what extent is it necessary to adopt the English conventions of this genre in order to be accepted and recognized by international communities? ⑨ This issue will be discussed in connection with the pedagogical implications arising from the findings and observations of this study.

A. As a genre with specific features of "interestingness" created to appeal to reviewing committees, the conference abstract has been attracting some scholarly attention. However, the issue of cultural variation in this genre has not been addressed. This paper describes and interprets the differences among English, Ukrainian, and Russian conference abstracts. (50 words)

B. Conference abstracts (CAs) are an important "gatekeeping" genre with interesting promotional features. Although these features are known in general terms, cross-cultural preferences and modifications have been little studied. Here, I compare English CAs with those written by Ukrainian and Russian specialists and explain those differences in cultural and ideological terms. (50 words)

C. The conference abstract is a common and important genre that plays a significant role in disseminating new knowledge within scientific communities. This paper describes the culture-specific differences of English versus Ukrainian and Russian conference abstracts. It then provides an explanation of the cultural and ideological backgrounds underlying these differences. (50 words)

Do you think the author needs a fourth version? If so, why?

Task Thirty-Two

Reduce your conference abstract to 50 words, or to the length expected in conference programs in your field. Notice that Tatyana's CA was impersonal: *this study, it will be shown.* Her short program abstracts A and C keep with *This paper*, but in B, she switches to *I.* Would this be an option for you?

PhD Dissertation Abstracts

One rather special type of abstract is the dissertation abstract (DA).[1] One reason for its special status is that at many U.S. research universities, it is a separately examined part of the dissertation. On a typical graduate school evaluation form, there is a separate line for the abstract where committee members are asked to check off one of the following.

_____ acceptable as submitted

_____ acceptable after minor typographical corrections

_____ acceptable after minor substantive revisions

_____ acceptable after major substantive revisions

_____ not acceptable

---

[1] We follow U.S. terminology—Master's theses but PhD dissertations. This terminology is often different elsewhere. The DA is also special because hardly anybody writes more than one!

One potential source of difficulty comes from the fact that *Proquest Information and Learning* (formerly UMI) "publishes" in digital or microfilm format PhD dissertations from many U.S. universities and, increasingly, PhD theses from other countries. As part of this service, the company requires a dissertation abstract of no more than 350 words. Given that dissertations represent large amounts of research and scholarship, getting the text down to this word limit can often be a frustrating task. As might be predicted, one common problem with early DA drafts is that too much space is taken up with the introductory matter and an outline of methods, leaving insufficient room to do justice to the findings and their implications.

At least in some fields, especially when the described work is interdisciplinary or multidisciplinary, there can also be a problem in making the abstract accessible (at least in part) to scholars (and even examiners) who might have a more marginal or incidental interest in the study. This aspect can be especially difficult for dissertation writers, who are, understandably, extremely closely involved in their research projects. It is not surprising then that chairs, committee members, and even friends often work with the candidate to finalize the abstract, frequently prior to, sometimes at, and sometimes after the oral defense.

Finally, the dissertation writers are often eager to promote their work, while advisors may wish to moderate the claims being made. Or indeed, the opposite situation can arise!

Task Thirty-Three

Here are the openings to three versions of the same dissertation abstract. The dissertation is from the field of occupational health and dealt with health issues arising from heavy computer use. Which, in your opinion, were the first, next, and final versions? (Sample answers for the tasks can be found in the *Commentary* at www.press.umich.edu/esl/compsite/ETRW/.)

Version A

The expanding utilization of computers in the workplace has made the VDT-related musculoskeletal disorders a growing concern.

Version B

The expanding utilization of computer technology in the workplace has made VDT-related musculoskeletal disorders one of the fastest growing concerns in the field of occupational health.

Version C

This dissertation presents three studies aimed at reducing the intensity or duration of static exertion to alleviate the musculoskeletal discomfort associated with intensive keyboarding operations.

An abstract for a dissertation in which John was involved follows. The study was interdisciplinary, involving techniques of discourse analysis from linguistics along with document collection and interview protocols from business communications. As a result, the dissertation was co-chaired by a linguist and a professor of business communications.

Task Thirty-Four

Read the abstract and answer the questions that follow. Work with a partner if possible. Part of this dissertation abstract will be familiar to you from Task Six.

Patterns and variations in contemporary written business communications in Turkey: A genre study of four companies

by Didar Akar

Co-chairs: Priscilla S. Rogers and John M. Swales

① This dissertation examines the discourse properties of contemporary Turkish commercial correspondence. ② The primary data used consist of approximately 450 memoranda (internal correspondence) and fax messages (external correspondence) associated with four different Turkish companies selected to represent a range of sectors, sizes and management styles. ③ The text and discourse analyses are supported by text-based interviews with informants from these companies.

④ The linguistic analysis is first framed within the socio-historical context of the emergence of the private sector in Turkey, and then within recent linguistic and literacy trends, and finally within the context of corporate cultures. ⑤ These frames of contextualization reveal how corporate culture can affect certain aspects of communicative practice, while also indicating that certain other aspects are inherently Turkish. ⑥ One particularly strong general influence in the memoranda came from public sector bureaucratic styles.

⑦ The rhetorical analysis focuses mainly on requests in both memoranda and fax messages. ⑧ Requests in Turkish are shown to be highly impersonal and relatively indirect. ⑨ Although the particular strategies preferred for internal or external communication vary, politeness strategies typically depersonalize the requests by avoiding reference to the receiver's agent status; as a result, the company emerges as a discourse participant which is, at times, more prominent than the sender or receiver. ⑩ On a syntactic level, one consequence is the heavy use made of passivization, nominalization, and particles such as {-DIr}. ⑪ On a discoursal level, postponement of a message's main communicative purpose following extensive groundwork appears as a common rhetorical pattern. ⑫ Emerging differences evolving away from the traditional arrangements and styles of business communication were found in fax messages, especially in the smaller companies, due to factors such as audience, means of delivery and types of intertextuality. ⑬ The dissertation closes by exploring the implications of this study for genre theory, and for teaching business communication courses in Turkish universities and corporate settings.

1. The title took (as usual!) a long time to finalize. As far as the committee was aware, this was the first real study of Turkish business language. Didar wanted to appeal to three groups with her title: (1) specialists in the Turkish language, (2) experts in (cross-cultural) business communications, and (3) linguists concerned with discourse. For this last group, she was particularly interested in getting the word *genre* into the title, partly because it was currently in theoretical fashion and partly because she thought she had an important theoretical point to make. The use of the word *genre* would also help link her specialized and "off-center" study to the wider field.

   Do you think Didar succeeded in making an appeal to her three groups?

2. Sentence 1 is a short, simple opening sentence that offers a summary of the dissertation. It could have started otherwise, of course. For example:

   Little is known about Turkish business language.

   Turkey is a growing economic power straddling Europe and Asia.

   Do you think Didar chose the right opening? And if so, why?

   The sentence in fact opens with a piece of metadiscourse *(This dissertation),* as does Version C in the previous task. The first verb is in the present tense *(examines)* and, as you will have noted, this tense predominates.

   Do you agree with these decisions?

3. In earlier drafts, Sentence 2 provided the exact number of memoranda and faxes, but this was replaced by an approximation.

   What are the advantages and disadvantages of this decision?

4. Sentence 2 states that *four different Turkish companies [were] selected to represent a range of sectors, sizes and management styles.* This statement is in fact one of those *post hoc* (after the fact) rationalizations. In reality, the "selection" of companies was opportunistic in that Didar relied on personal contacts. It just happened that the people she knew worked in different kinds of companies.

   Should she have expressed this differently? Perhaps more true to fact?

5. Sentence 3 is all that remains of an earlier paragraph that described the various methods of analysis. These methods are now referred to one by one in the third paragraph (rhetorical, syntactic, discoursal, etc.) within the context of *results.*

   Would you have preferred more on methods?

6. Notice that Sentence 5 opens with *These frames of contextualization. . . .*

   What kind of subject is this nice summary phrase? (See the first Language Focus on pages 11–12.)

7. In Sentence 6, we find the first use of a past tense. Why?

   In Sentence 8, the finding is expressed pretty strongly *(Requests . . . are shown to be . . . as opposed to, say, Requests tend to be . . .).* Why?

   (Hint: What might be the expected form of written American business requests?)

9. Notice that Sentences 10 and 11 respectively open with *On a syntactic level . . .* and *On a discoursal level. . . .*

   What is the effect of this rhetorical device (parallel structure)?

10. Just as the abstract opened with a metadiscoursal reference to itself, so the final sentence begins with the same tactic. Note this time, however, that the demonstrative *this* has been replaced by the definite article *the.*

    Is this clever?

   Now, here is a second DA to consider, this time from 2005. It also comes from the University of Michigan, where it won a highly competitive Distinguished Dissertation Award. The field is Archaeology, the location is Egypt, and the time is the centuries immediately proceeding the CE (current era). We have added a map to indicate the roads investigated as well as a number of explanatory notes.

Task Thirty-Five

Read the text, and complete the tasks that follow.

Figure 4. Map of Egypt with Ptolemaic and Roman Routes through the Eastern Desert

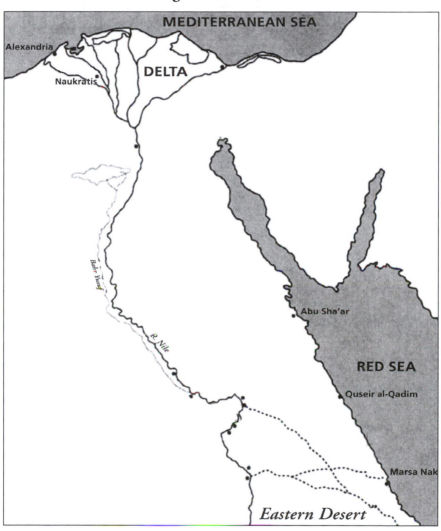

Traveling the desert edge: The Ptolemaic[a] roadways and regional economy of Egypt's Eastern Desert[b] in the fourth through first centuries BCE

Jennifer E. Gates
(Co-chairs: Susan E. Alcock & Sharon C. Herbert)

(1) The present study is the first archaeologically-based examination of the economic and cultural dynamics of Egypt's Eastern Desert in the Hellenistic[c] period (332–31 BCE). (2) Using unpublished archaeological material in an investigation of this understudied region, it offers a more diverse conceptualization of ancient economic practice at the regional level and the intersection of the Ptolemaic economy with other cultural factors. (3) This investigation emerged in response to long-standing notions about the conquest and subsequent colonization of Egypt by Greeks in the Hellenistic Period.

(4) Drawing on extensive archaeological survey undertaken since 1992 and independent ceramic analysis,[d] this project brings together the material evidence for a road network in the southern half of Egypt's Eastern Desert, which was part of a developing system of long-distance trade and transport implemented during the Hellenistic period. (5) This study provides a chronology of settlement, site use and abandonment that for the first time illuminates the intensity and scale of developments in the Eastern Desert under the Ptolemies. (6) These conclusions are the result of a re-dating of the ceramic sequence[e] from the Eastern Desert and a reconsideration of settlement and travel patterns along these trade routes. (7) Taken with the limited historical and papyrological[f] material from this region, these new insights suggest a highly variable chronology of usage along the desert roads and considerable flexibility in the economic and administrative arrangements in the region.

(8) Although foregrounding the economic implications of this material, this study also takes the Eastern Desert under consideration from an innovative cultural history perspective. (9) The model resulting from the

archaeological investigations is weighed in conjunction with an analysis of the real and 'imagined' landscape of southern Egypt, as articulated by Greek geographers and travel-writers[g] during the sixth through first centuries BCE. (10) Taken with the patterns revealed by the archaeological study, an analysis of these sources suggests that, although resource acquisition and economic gain were undoubtedly important reasons for desert settlement, the exploration of the Eastern Desert during the Hellenistic period was likely influenced by an interest in documenting exotic and liminal[h] portions of the Ptolemaic countryside during the third and second centuries BCE.

(347 words!)

Notes

[a] *Ptolemaic* (the 'p' is not pronounced): The Ptolemies ruled Egypt from around 300 BCE to 30 BCE. They were Greek in origin.

[b] The Eastern Desert is to the east of the Nile and the Western Desert to the river's west.

[c] a mixture of Greek and Near Eastern cultures that came together in the Middle East following the conquests of Alexander the Great

[d] study of ancient earthenware pots and shards (broken pieces of pots)

[e] a dated ordering of ceramic material

[f] paper made out of reeds and used for writing on; *papyrology:* the study of ancient Egyptian documents written on papyri

[g] The most famous of these was Herodutus

[h] on the boundary

Part A

We contacted the author by email and she answered our questions as follows. As you read the replies, mark them to indicate whether you were (VS) very surprised, (SS) somewhat surprised, or (NS) not surprised by what she had to say.

1. Did the abstract and title easily pass the defense or was there further work to be done?

    _____ There were no requests for revisions to the abstract at the defense stage, or at any stage, that I can recall.

2. Was it basically your own text or did the co-chairs help out?

    _____ It was entirely my own text, with no input from either.

3. The abstract seems pitched fairly broadly (i.e., not to a super-specialized audience); was that deliberate?

_____ Yes, I wrote it to appeal to a broad archaeological and historical audience, since I imagined it would be most useful as a vehicle for getting people interested in the dissertation, rather than speaking to specialists who were already interested in the topic.

4. The abstract goes to some length to emphasize various novel elements in your study. Was it your idea to adopt this strategy, or was the committee involved?

_____ Again, this was my idea and part of how I felt I needed to present my research, generally. . . . I tried to emphasize the innovative aspects of the project and ways that it might offer new and challenging perspectives on the material. I felt that this would help distinguish the dissertation (in a reasonable way) from the mountains of others out there, and I genuinely felt that some of the things that were "new" were some of the most important things that I did in the project.

5. What are your feelings about your title? If you were to turn your dissertation into a book, would you change it?

_____ I would most definitely change it. It's a deadly dull title! I really struggled with coming up with a title that didn't sound ridiculous. It's consistently the thing that I struggle with most on any project, whether it's an article, dissertation or book project. . . .

Part B
Review the abstract, highlighting all words and phrases that underscore novelty and newsworthiness. What might you conclude? If relevant, would you anticipate a similar strategy for your own DA?

Most academics only write one dissertation abstract, even if some go on to help their own students with theirs. Therefore, only do 1, 2, or 3 in this next task if it is relevant to your situation.

Task Thirty-Six

1. Find and photocopy a dissertation abstract from your own field. Rhetorically and organizationally, how is it similar to or different from the one discussed in Task Thirty-Five? If there are major differences, what explanations would you have?

2. Contact a recent graduate from your department and ask him or her by email the kinds of questions we asked Jennifer Gates.

3. Again if it is relevant to your situation, write a draft abstract for your PhD dissertation or thesis. If you are outside of the United States, follow your local rules for length, layout, and so on. (See the Appendix for comments on the Russian "autoreferat.")

We have now worked through all the major types of abstracts. The remaining task is to choose a suitable list of keywords for your RA abstract.

Choosing Keywords

Journals are increasingly requiring authors to submit a short list of keywords or key phrases (also sometimes known as *indexing terms*) along with the rest of their papers.[1] Usually, four to eight such items are requested, although up to ten are sometimes permitted in the sciences. Keywords are used to provide efficient indexing, search, and retrieval mechanisms as articles become available through electronic systems. Misleading or uninformative keywords can adversely affect the uptake of your work. A few journals state that the keywords should not appear in the title (e.g., *Written Communication, Economics and Developmental Studies*), but most are silent on this issue.

Task Thirty-Seven

Here, once again, is the first abstract discussed (on page 3). Of the following list, choose the three or four most appropriate keywords or phrases. (Sample answers for these tasks can be found in the *Commentary* at www.press.umich. edu/esl/compsite/ETRW/.)

Keywords: scholars; democracy; welfare; poverty; child mortality; non-democratic states; cross-national studies; money; benefits; government expenditure; comparison

Abstract

① Many scholars claim that democracy improves the welfare of the poor. ② This article uses data on infant and child mortality to challenge this claim. ③ Cross-national studies tend to exclude from their samples non-democratic states that have performed well; this leads to the mistaken inference that non-democracies have worse records than democra-

---

[1] For U.S. dissertations, ProQuest states that keywords are not required, but they will be added if not submitted.

cies. ④ Once these and other flaws are corrected, democracy has little or no effect on infant and child mortality rates. ⑤ Democracies spend more money on education and health than non-democracies, but these benefits seem to accrue to middle- and upper-income groups.

Now, here are some further pointers toward producing a professional list of keywords.

Check the keywords used in your reference collection of abstracts:

1. Are there keywords at all?

2. If so, how many keywords or key phrases are typically provided?

3. What are the common keywords?

4. Are some of the keywords the same as the words used in the title? And is this a good idea?

5. Are any too general to be useful?

6. Are they listed alphabetically, or based on the author's perception of their importance?

7. Is capitalization used at all?

8. What punctuation is used between the keywords?

Look up the website for your favorite journal or journals. What advice is given about keywords? In particular, check whether your favorite journal or journals actually provide a list of keywords to choose from. For example, the *Journal of Alloys and Compounds,* the *Journal of Applied Logic,* and the *Journal of Operations Management* all provide keyword lists.

Task Thirty-Eight

Construct a careful list of keywords for one of your own abstracts.

Appendix:
Notes on Cross-Linguistic Issues

References to Your Longer Text

In English, these are typically *this paper* (which does not easily translate) and *this article* (which usually does). But note that there are some cross-cultural preferences here: Spanish speakers often opt for *trabajo* (work) (Reinhart, 2007), while Arabic speakers prefer *baHth* (research). The direct translations of these are rarely used in English abstracts.

Cross-Cultural Comparisons

As shown in Task Twelve (page 25), English language RA abstracts are today often required for articles written in other languages—doubtless in an attempt to bring the summarized findings to a broader audience. Sarah Van Bonn and John recently completed a study of paired English and French RA abstracts in a language science journal published in France. They found that 24 of the 30 paired abstracts were very similar; in other words, the original language (whether French or English) had simply been translated into the target language. In the remaining 20 percent, however, the authors radically changed their English language abstracts. Among the changes noted were:

- Leaving out local details only relevant to academics in France
- Focusing more on theory rather than local teaching concerns
- Splitting long French sentences into two
- Using a more informal style (e.g., opting for *I* or *we*)

Task Thirty-Nine

Write a short abstract of one of your current projects in your first language for a local journal. Translate it into English for a wider audience, making any changes you think appropriate. Write up a short commentary on any changes that you made and why you made them.

Dissertation Abstracts in Russia and Other Ex-Soviet Union Countries

In Russia and other countries of the former Soviet Union, every dissertation has to be preceded by a so-called *автореферат* (autoreferat). The autoreferat is a stand-alone document that provides a general description of the dissertation, presenting it to the dissertation committee and a wider audience. It is submitted to all committee members as well as to other parties potentially interested in the research (such as academic institutions, organizations, or companies) at least a month before the scheduled defense date. A permission to submit an autoreferat is seen as the final step before the dissertation defense.

Our assistant Vera's survey of autoreferats from a number of fields showed that the average length of such documents (excluding the list of author's publications that differed in length from author to author) was about 5,600 words but varied widely. However, each of the autoreferats followed a similar structure, basically containing the following sections:

1. General description of the dissertation, including
   - the timeliness of the research
   - research goals
   - methodology used in the dissertation
   - main results presented for the defense
   - scholarly novelty and merit
   - practical merit
   - structure and the size of the dissertation, indicating its length, number of chapters, figures, tables, references, etc.
2. Dissertation structure (chapter by chapter), including main formulas, figures, and tables

3. Explanation of main results and conclusions of the research

4. Detailed list of author's publications on the topic of the dissertation

Besides committee members and interested parties, the autoreferat is also sent to the so-called "opponents" (experts in the field appointed to challenge your research findings during the dissertation defense). In this case, the autoreferat is accompanied by a letter asking for feedback, designed to help the author prepare for the dissertation defense.

Sources

Akar, D. (1998). Patterns and variations in contemporary written business communications in Turkey: A genre study of four companies. Doctoral dissertation, University of Michigan, Ann Arbor.

Barro, J. R., & Cutler, D. M. (1997). Consolidation in the medical care marketplace: A case study from Massachusetts. *NBER Working Papers* W5957.

Carnegie, G. D., & Walker, S. P. (2007). Household accounting in Australia: Prescription and practice from the 1820s to the 1960s. *Accounting, Auditing and Accountability Journal, 20*(1), 41–73.

Elias, M. S., Cano, M. A., & Mestriner Júnior, W. (2001). The importance of buccal health for adolescents of different social strata of Ribeirão Preto. *Revista Latino-Americana de Enfermagem, 9*(1), 88–95.

Ellman, P. I., Law, M. G., Tache-Leon, C., Reece, B. T., Maxey, T. S., Peeler, B. B., et al. (2004). Sleep deprivation does not affect operative results in cardiac surgery. Paper presented at Fortieth Annual Meeting of the Society of Throacic Surgeons, San Antonio, TX.

Gates, J. E. (2005). Traveling the desert edge: The Ptolemaic roadways and regional economy of Egypt's Eastern Desert in the fourth through first centuries. Doctoral dissertation, University of Michigan, Ann Arbor.

Giles, H., & Kim, K.-H. (2006). Transparent façade panel typologies based on hybrid bio-composite and recyclable polymer materials. Paper presented at ARCC/EAAE International Conference, Temple University, Philadelphia, PA.

Griffeth, R. W., Gaertner, S. & Sager, J. K. (1999). Taxonomic model of withdrawal behaviours: The adaptive response model. *Human Resource Management Review, 9*(4), 577–590.

Hand, I. L., Kim, M., Yoon, J. J., Noble, L., & North, A. (2006). Psychiatric symptoms among postpartum women in an urban hospital setting. *American Journal of Perinatology, 23*(6), 329–334.

Hartley, J. (2004). Current findings from research on structures abstracts. *Journal of Medical Library Association, 92*(3), 368–371.

Heathcote, J. A. (1995). Why do old men have big ears? *British Medical Journal, 311,* 1668–1669.

Huang, I.-W. (1999). Effects of keyboards, armrests, and alternating keying positions on subjective discomfort and preferences among data entry operators. Doctoral dissertation, University of Michigan, Ann Arbor.

Magnuson, K. A., Rohm, C. & Waldfogel, J. (2007). Does prekindergarten improve school preparation and performance? *Economics of Education Review, 26,* 33–51.

Pike, D. (2005). Collision rules for high-speed craft. *Journal of Navigation, 58,* 159–163.

Räisänen, C. (1999). *The conference forum as a system of genres.* Göteborg, Sweden: Acta Universitatis Gothoburgensis.

Ross, M. (2006). Is democracy good for the poor? *American Journal of Political Science, 50*(4), 860–874.

Saleem, Q., Wildman, R. D., Huntley, J. M., & Whitworth, M. B. (2003). A novel application of speckle interferometry for the measurement of strain distributions in semi-sweet biscuits. *Measurement in Science and Technology, 14*(12), 2027–2033.

Spennemann, D. H. R. (2004). The occurrence of owls in the Marshall Islands. *Notornis, 51,* 147–151.

Walczak, G. (2007). Low art, popular imagery and civic commitment in the French revolution. *Art History, 30*(2), 247–277.

Yakhontova, T. (1998). Cultural variation in the genre of the conference abstract: Rhetorical and linguistic dimensions. Paper presented at the Conference on English as a Conference Language, Halle-Wittenberg, Germany.

Young, J. & Buchanan, N. (1996). Antiracist/multicultural teacher education: A focus on student teachers. Research notes. *Alberta Journal of Educational Research, 42*(1), 60–64.

References

Bazerman, C. (1988). *Shaping written knowledge: The genre and activity of the experimental article in science.* Madison: University of Wisconsin Press.

Berkenkotter, C., & Huckin, T. N. (1995). *Genre knowledge in disciplinary communication.* Hillsdale, NJ: Lawrence Erlbaum.

Bordage, G., & McCaghie. W. C. (2001). Title, authors, and abstracts. *Academic Medicine, 76*(9), 945–947.

Hartley, J. (2004). Current findings from research on structured abstracts. *Journal of the Medical Library Association, 92*(3), 368–371.

Hartley, J. (2007). There's more to the title than meets the eye: Exploring possibilities. *Journal of Technical Writing and Communication, 37*(1): 95–101.

Huckin, T. N. (2001). Abstracting from abstracts. In M. Hewings (Ed.), *Academic writing in context,* Birmingham, UK: University of Birmingham Press.

Hyland, K. (2004). *Disciplinary discourses: Social interactions in academic writing. Michigan Classics Edition.* Ann Arbor: University of Michigan Press.

Hyland, K., & Tse, P. (2005). Hooking the reader: A corpus study of evaluative *that* in abstracts. *English for Specific Purposes, 24*(2), 123–139.

Langdon-Neuner, E. (2008). Hangings at the BMJ: What editors discuss when deciding to accept or reject research papers. *The Write Stuff, 17*(2), 84–86.

Mauranen, A. (1993). *Cultural differences in academic rhetoric: A textlinguistic study.* Frankfurt: Peter Lang.

Orasan, C. (2001). Patterns in scientific abstracts. Paper presented at Corpus Linguistics Conference, Lancaster University, Lancaster, UK.

Reinhart, S. M. (2007). An analysis of purpose statements in abstracts in English from a Venezuelan dental journal. Poster presented at PPRISEAL conference (Publishing and Presenting Research Internationally: Issues for Speakers of English as an Additional Language), University of La Laguna, Tenerife, Spain.

Van Bonn, S., & Swales, J. (2007). English and French journal abstracts in the language sciences: Three exploratory studies. *Journal of English for Academic Purposes, 6,* 93–108.